THE
LIVERPOOL
BOOK
OF
DAYS

STEVEN HORTON

All sources acknowledged in text except websites (various) and the following:

McIlwee, Michael, *The Gangs of Liverpool: From the Cornermen to the High Rip – The Mobs that Terrorised a City*, Milo Books, 2006

France, David and Prentice, David, *Dr Everton's Magnificent Obsession*, Trinity Mirror Sport Media, 2008

Munro, Alasdair and Sim, Duncan, *The Merseyside Scots: A Study of an Expatriate Community*, Liver Press, 2001

Hand, C.R., *Olde Liverpool and its Charter*, 1907

Peet, Henry, *Thomas Steers: The Engineer of Liverpool's First Dock. A Memoir*, 1932

Pye, Ken, *Discover Liverpool*, Trinity Mirror North West and North Wales, 2011

McCarron, Ken and Jarvis, Adrian, *Give a Dock a Good Name?* Merseyside Port Folios, 1992

First published 2012

The History Press
The Mill, Brimscombe Port
Stroud, Gloucestershire, GL5 2QG
www.thehistorypress.co.uk

British Library Cataloguing in Publication Data.
A catalogue record for this book is available from the British Library.

ISBN 978 0 7524 7111 2

Typesetting and origination by The History Press
Printed in India

JANUARY 1ST

1847: On this day, Dr William Henry Duncan was appointed as Liverpool's Medical Officer for Health, the first position of its kind in the country. Dr Duncan was born to Scottish parents in Seel Street, and after completing his medical studies in Edinburgh he returned to Liverpool to practice as a GP.

In 1843 he produced a pamphlet, *The Physical Causes of the High Mortality Rate in Liverpool*, which showed how disease was linked to living conditions. It led to the 1846 Liverpool Sanitary Act, which paved the way for the creation of the post.

The *Liverpool Mercury* welcomed Duncan's appointment, commenting on 5 January:

> The appointment of Dr Duncan as Medical Officer is one which does credit to the Council, for that gentleman was one of the first to take up the sanitary question and has since been one of the most active and persevering advocates.

Duncan worked closely with Liverpool's Borough Engineer James Newlands over the seventeen years he held the position to improve living and sanitary conditions in the town.

January 2nd

1976: Liverpool was hit by hurricane-force winds that topped 115mph, causing chaos and devastation.

On the River Mersey a supertanker carrying 43,000 tons of crude oil broke from its moorings at Tranmere and drifted across the river, eventually running aground in low tide. Trains were cancelled and flights diverted, whilst in Seaforth two cranes collided after one was cut loose from its rails.

The *Daily Post* the following day described it as 'the worst night on the River Mersey in living memory', continuing its report with an account of the damage caused:

> Cross river ferry services were suspended and balance gangways on the floating landing stage at Liverpool Pier Head were smashed as they lowered onto the decks of the ferry boats. The stage and pier head were flooded. Across Merseyside chimney stacks blew off, trees fell and power went down.

The following day, as the clean-up operation began, the landing stage, which had only been built six months earlier, sank under the weight of the water, leading to the cancellation of more ferry services as the salvage operation began.

JANUARY 3RD

1641: Astronomer Jeremiah Horrocks, the first person to observe the transit of Venus across the Sun, died suddenly in Toxteth Park.

The son of a farmer, he had gone to Cambridge University but not formally graduated as he couldn't afford to continue his studies. As a curate, he continued his scientific studies, correctly predicting and observing the transit of Venus across the Sun in 1639. He also studied the orbit of the Moon and tides and may have become as famous as Galileo had he not died so prematurely. After he died, he was buried in the Ancient Chapel of Toxteth in Park Road. His death was described by fellow astronomer William Crabtree as an 'incalculable loss'.

A marble stone in Westminster Abbey in his honour reads:

In memory of Jeremiah Horrocks, curate of Hoole, in Lancashire, who died on the 3rd of January 1641, in or near his 22nd year; Having in so short a life detected the long inequality in the mean motion of Jupiter and Saturn; Discovered the orbit of the moon to be an ellipse; Determined the motion of the lunar apse; Suggested the physical cause of its revolution; And predicted from his own observations the transit of Venus, which was seen by himself and his friend, William Crabtree, on Sunday the 24th November 1639.

JANUARY 4TH

1875: two men were hanged at Kirkdale Jail for the brutal murder of a man in Tithebarn Street the previous August Bank Holiday.

On that day, twenty-six-year-old dock worker Robert Morgan had been to New Brighton with his wife and brother. Whilst walking down Tithebarn Street he was asked for money by seventeen-year-old John McCrave. Morgan suggested that he should work if he wanted money for drink, at which point he was set upon by McCrave and two companions, Peter Campbell and Michael Mullen. They punched him to the ground before kicking him 40ft down the road like a football.

All three youths were tried and sentenced to death, but Campbell was reprieved on account of his previous good character. He was only told this news two days before the scheduled execution in the presence of McCrave and Mullen, who were reported in the *Liverpool Mercury* to have cried bitterly on confirmation of their own fate.

The day after the execution, the *Liverpool Mercury* reported: 'McCrave looked up to the rope and then the white cap was placed over his face and the rope around his neck. He appeared to tremble violently and in a tremulous voice repeated "Lord, have mercy on me". Mullen conducted himself more quietly.'

JANUARY 5TH

1947: The Lord Mayor of Liverpool was subject to a savage verbal attack by a fellow councillor over the proposed opening of cinemas on Sundays.

The Sunday Entertainments Act (1932) allowed local councils to use their own discretion as to whether or not to grant licences for cinemas to open. Liverpool Council was considering the move to stop youths getting involved in trouble on the streets.

Lord Mayor Alderman W.G. Gregson was on a state visit to the City Temple in Catharine Street on this particular Sunday when the Revd H.D. Longbottom, who was a councillor for the Liverpool Protestant Party, launched his tirade during his sermon.

The next day's *Daily Post* reported that he opened by saying he made no apologies for bringing his views up during a state visit and warned that he would have more alarming and outspoken things to say in the future. He then went on to say:

> I hope we shall not be misled by stories that this Sunday opening
> is in the interests of the youth in this city. It is in the interests of
> the money bags behind the cinema. I cannot understand some
> Christian people who think you can twist the commitments of
> God to please popular taste.

JANUARY 6TH

1908: Today seven-year-old Madge Kirby disappeared from her home in Kensington, never to be seen alive again. It is a murder mystery that remains unsolved.

On 11 January the *Liverpool Mercury* reported the disappearance under the headline 'MYSTERIOUS DISAPPEARANCE OF A LIVERPOOL CHILD':

> Liverpool police are investigating the remarkable case of a child's disappearance so far without success. Margaret T. Kirby aged 7 years, residing with her father David Kirby, a plumber, at 55 Romilly Street Kensington, her mother died only a few weeks ago. About half past four on Monday afternoon Margaret was with her brother three years of age in Farnworth Street off Kensington when they were accosted by a strange man who asked the girl if she would go for some sweets. Child-like she obeyed with alacrity, from that moment to the present the girl has not been heard of. The girl has dark brown hair, blue eyes, a prominent nose and fresh completion and when she was last seen was dressed in a black shirt worn at the sleeves, blue pinafore, black velvet bonnet with black strings, black stockings with black boots.

It was seven months before Margaret's fate was confirmed when a sack containing her badly decomposed body was found in Great Newton Street. Margaret was buried in Ford Cemetery with her mother and tragically her father died just six weeks afterwards, unable to cope with the grief. Her killer was never caught.

JANUARY 7TH

1901: James Dunwoody Bulloch, a Liverpool based agent for the Confederates during the American Civil War, died.

Bulloch, originally from Savannah, Georgia, had arrived in Liverpool in 1861 with a brief to secure funds and contracts for the building of warships. With the UK being neutral, he had to convince the authorities that his ships were solely for merchant purposes, and despite being watched closely by the US consul and customs officials, he was always able to stay one step ahead. His most famous ship was the raider *Alabama*, which was built at Cammell Laird in 1862 and captured over sixty-five Union ships.

The war finished in 1865 and Bulloch remained in Liverpool, living in Sefton Park and trading as a cotton merchant. The day after he died of cancer of the rectum and cardiac failure his death notice in the *Liverpool Mercury* read:

> January 7th at 76 Canning Street (the residence of his son in law M. H. Maxwell jun) aged 77 years, James Dunwoody Bulloch, late of Savannah, Georgia, USA and formerly naval representative of the Confederate States in Europe during the Civil War. Funeral Service at St Margaret's church, Princes Road on Thursday next at 10.45 a.m., internment at Smithdown Road cemetery, 11.15 a.m.

His funeral was attended by Captain John Low from the *Alabama* and his gravestone carries the inscription, 'An American by Birth, an Englishman by Choice'.

January 8th

1983: A new musical written by Willy Russell, *Blood Brothers*, premiered at the Liverpool Playhouse.

The play, about twin brothers separated at birth who go on to have very different social backgrounds and then fall in love with the same girl, was based loosely on the 1844 novel *The Corsican Brothers* by Alexandre Dumas.

In the *Liverpool Echo* on 10 January, theatre critic Joe Riley was full of praise, writing:

> Take a commonplace issue, forge it in the white heat of growing social awareness and then present it to the world, via Merseyside, as a masterly piece of theatre. It is a triumph for all concerned. For Barbara Dickson, there's much deserved acclaim for her first singing-acting role as the mother. She really gets to the show's emotional heart in a most beguiling way; a London transfer should be assured. In the meantime make a Playhouse ticket a certainty for yourselves.

The *Daily Mail*'s Patrick O'Neill wrote:

> It may be a little early for prophecy, but I rashly predict that come December this extraordinary show will be among the best new musicals of 1983.

The predictions from the reviews were not wrong. Since its Playhouse beginnings the show has toured all over the world, including New York's Broadway, and has been running permanently in London's West End since 1988.

JANUARY 9TH

1941: Liverpool suffered heavy bombing raids by German warplanes, with twenty residents of Virgil Street in Everton losing their lives.

There had been some bomber activity earlier in the month but – apart from stables being damaged in Newsham Park – no major incidents. This particular night, however, the docks were heavily bombed, with houses in Everton and South Liverpool also being hit. The biggest tragedy was at 32 Virgil Street, where four children under seven were killed.

Those that died in Virgil Street were:

John Abbot, age fifty-seven
John Adams, age two
Mary Adams, age twenty-six
George Butterworth, age six
James Butterworth, age one
Brian Butterworth, age three
Joan Butterworth, age seven
Mary Carlisle, age forty-six
Catherine Hodge, age four
Elizabeth Jackson, age fifty-seven

Mary Jones, age seventy-two
Elizabeth McHenry, age sixteen
Claire McKevitt, age thirteen
John McKevitt, age nineteen
Joseph McKevitt, age fifty-seven
Teresa McKevitt, age sixteen
James Parker, age seventy-seven
William Parker, age sixty-nine
Joan Smith, age twenty-six
John Smith, age five

The full extent of the raid couldn't be mentioned in the press due to reporting restrictions. The next night's *Liverpool Echo* described 'extensive damage to houses' and stated: 'Altogether casualties were amazingly light considering the length of the raid and number of bombs dropped'.

JANUARY 10TH

1922: Shipping magnate and philanthropist John Rankin was today given the Freedom of Liverpool.

Rankin had donated generously to the University of Liverpool and Liverpool Cathedral and was accompanied by his wife and two sons to the ceremony. It was held in a committee room to ensure it remained low key (due to his failing health).

The following day's *Daily Post* reported that the Lord Mayor said in his opening address: 'The highest honour in its gift has been bestowed on men of imperial note and men eminent in civic service and philanthropy, but in no case had the consensus of approval been more pronounced than in the case of the gentleman they were now honouring.'

Rankin was presented with an illuminated scroll and silver tea tray by Sir Archibald Savidge, Leader of the Council. The *Post* reported how Rankin: 'In accepting the honour and the gift said that he found it difficult to adequately express his feelings on receiving this highest of privileges. He felt heartfelt pride that a citizen and merchant received it as he hadn't given great service to the country like others before him.'

JANUARY 11TH

1892: Liverpool Central underground station opened today.

The Mersey Railway was built in 1886, connecting Birkenhead and Liverpool, terminating at James Street and the new extensions were to Central and Rock Ferry. The evening edition of the *Liverpool Echo* reported that: 'Bookings on the new section if the Mersey Railway were this morning very satisfactory, many business people availing themselves of the extension, and others doing so in a vein of curiosity.'

The *Echo* stated that journey times between Central and Rock Ferry were fifteen minutes, with certain peak time trains being only thirteen minutes. Today, the journey takes twelve minutes. The opening of Central Station was not without problems, as the *Echo* reported there were some delays due to steam getting in the tunnels, causing: 'Delay in the shunting and changing of engines, as the signals could not be seen distinctly. This however is a matter which it is expected will soon be put right. On the whole the working of the new extension was very satisfactory.'

Today Liverpool Central is Britain's busiest underground station outside London, carrying 18 million passengers a year.

JANUARY 12TH

1966: Drilling began on the Queensway (Wallasey) tunnel. That evening's *Liverpool Echo* reported:

> Wearing a yellow safety helmet the Lord Mayor, Alderman David Cowley inaugurated work on Merseyside's £20 million second tunnel this morning when he set the drilling machinery in motion at the site at Waterloo Dock Goods Depot for the boring of the first of five ventilation shafts. Watched by the Mayors of Birkenhead and Wallasey the Lord Mayor started drilling at 11.35am. Half an hour later the Mayor of Wallasey performed a similar ceremony on the Wallasey side at a site in Tudor Avenue near the Seacombe ferry. This morning's ceremonies were the culmination of years of discussions, sometimes arguments, about a second crossing.

Even with completion of the new tunnel some five years away, the *Echo* suggested that even more would come. It reported that a third tunnel was envisaged as taking traffic under the Mersey well to the south of the present tunnel and that with the growth of traffic it was possible that yet more crossings would be needed before the century was out.

JANUARY 13TH

1974: The Football League Management Committee paved the way for Sunday football, leading to a mixed response from Merseyside clubs.

The UK was in the grip of an energy crisis, leading to the 'three day week' to save electricity. The Football League decided to allow Sunday games as they would put less of a strain on the National Grid than games on Saturdays. The previous week four FA Cup games had been played on a Sunday and attracted higher than average crowds.

The following day the *Daily Post* reported that Tranmere Rovers had already switched their next game with Aldershot to the Sunday but Liverpool were against the idea: 'Stoke are almost certain to ask Liverpool if they will be prepared to visit the Victoria Ground on Sunday instead of Saturday. Stoke are very much in the forefront of Sunday pioneers. But they will have to think again, Liverpool will have no part in it.'

A statement from the club added: 'These games must be switched by mutual consent and they will get no joy from us.'

Everton kept an open mind, stating that they wouldn't switch the following Saturday's game with Leeds as nearly all tickets had been sold but their overall attitude was one of wait and see for the future. On 27 January, they did play a Sunday game against West Bromwich Albion.

JANUARY 14TH

1907: Eleven ships' firemen were jailed for neglect of duty. Ships' firemen were required to maintain the fires that kept the boilers going and any failure to do their jobs could have serious implications in terms of maintaining schedules.

The *Liverpool Daily Courier* reported the next day under the headline 'DISOBEDIENT FIREMEN JAILED':

At the Liverpool Police Court yesterday before Mr W. J. Stewart Stipendiary Magistrate – Patrick O'Brien, Michael Slavin, George Duffy, James Birchall, Arthur Trainor, J. O'Brien, John Burns, J. Murphy, Patrick Cavanagh, Arthur Reardon and John Keeley were charged, on remand, on the information of Matthew Robertson, Master of the steamer *Ikbal* of the Welsford Line, with having combined together to neglect duty. Each of the prisoners was sentenced to one months' imprisonment, the Stipendiary Magistrate stating that conduct had occasioned a great waste of time for the ship.

January 15th

1864: A huge explosion on a boat on the River Mersey was felt all over Liverpool.

The following day's *Daily Post* reported under the headline 'TERRIFIC EXPLOSION YESTERDAY EVENING': 'Yesterday the people of Liverpool experienced an alarm greater than ever they had experienced before. A terrific shock was felt from one extremity of the town to another, and the first impression of all was that the house was tumbling down around them.'

There was speculation that there had been an earthquake or gas explosion, but it was soon apparent that the source was the *Lotty Sleigh*, which had eleven tons of gunpowder on board. The report went on:

> Soon after five o'clock the steward was cleaning a paraffin oil lamp. Through some inadvertence the oil was spilt on the floor and ignited. The crew were taken to the landing stage. Crowds were promptly attracted to the pier heads. Gradually the fire increased and at 7.20 p.m. the powder exploded. The mast flew up in the air, the ship disappeared into fragments and those who stood the concussion say that it was the most magnificent sight they had ever looked upon.

Windows all over town were blown out and the blast was heard as far away as Old Swan and West Derby. Miraculously, nobody was killed.

JANUARY 16TH

1870: The church of St Nicholas in Berkeley Street, Toxteth – more commonly known as the Liverpool Greek Orthodox church – was consecrated.

The church was only the second Greek Orthodox church to be built in England and was built in the Byzantine style, being very similar to St Theodore's church in Constantinople (now Istanbul). A Greek community had been in existence in Liverpool for nearly fifty years. Some of the first settlers had arrived from the island of Chios, following a massacre by Turkish forces in 1822 that saw half the population wiped out.

The church was consecrated by the Archbishop of Syra and Tinos Alexandros Lycourgos, who visited Liverpool especially for the occasion.

The next day the *Liverpool Mercury* reported that:

> Admission was obtained by ticket only, with nearly all the resident Greeks in Liverpool present, together with a number of their fellow countrymen from Manchester and London. The Archbishop removed the holy relics from the plate and placed them in a small silver case into which holy ointment had been poured. This was deposited in a hole cut in the top column of the holy table.

The church, now a Grade II listed building, remains a focal point for the Greek community in Liverpool.

JANUARY 17TH

1884: Almost exactly twenty years after the *Lotty Sleigh* exploded, there was another fire on the River Mersey when six boys carried out an arson attack on the *Clarence*, a reformatory ship.

The ship was a former navy vessel that was loaned by the Liverpool Catholic Reformatory Association in 1864, for boys who had served prison sentences to be trained in seamanship to reform their behaviour. The following day's *Liverpool Mercury* reported that the fire had begun at 2.15 p.m.: 'The crew and the boys tried every exertion to keep down the conflagration, which speedily raged with great fury. The water however had little or no effect on the fire. Captain Hudson gave directions for the boys to be taken ashore.'

At the time the cause of the fire was unknown but the *Mercury* appeared to have its suspicions, stating: 'It is said that a fire broke out in the same place Saturday last,' and 'we understand that for some time past considerable insubordination has been shown on board.'

When the fire was confirmed as an arson attack, those responsible were sentenced to six years' penal servitude. The following year a new *Clarence* was acquired to act as a reformatory – and also destroyed by fire in 1899.

January 18th

1795: Liverpool Town Hall was severely damaged by a fire. The fire occurred on a Sunday, the day after a council meeting at which some members believed they could smell burning, and it may well have been smouldering for several days between floors.

On Monday 19 January, *Billinge's Liverpool Advertiser* reported: 'We are sorry to inform the public that a very dreadful fire broke out yesterday morning within the council chamber of the exchange and raged with such violence as to consume the whole of the old part of the building, except the record room and treasurer's office.'

The *Advertiser* also included a statement from Mayor John Shaw, assuring the public that the records and material papers were in a perfect state of preservation and offering thanks to Major Clarkson and the Allies of the Southern Fencibles (army regiments raised to defend against a feared French invasion).

The fire meant the Mayor had to carry out his duties from a coffee room in Exchange Alley while the treasurer moved to an insurance office in Brunswick Street.

The re-constructed Town Hall was completed in 1802, and a new dome was added.

JANUARY 19TH

1886: There was a bizarre incident at the Royal Court Theatre when one actor assaulted another. The next day the *Daily Albion* reported:

> The rehearsal of *Nadesha* at the Royal Court Theatre by the Carl Rosa Opera Company on Tuesday was the occasion of a very extraordinary incident. At the time there were on the stage Colonel Mapleson, Mr Leslie Crotty and several members of the company. Colonel Mapleson alleges that Leslie Crotty went up to him whilst on the stage and struck him between the eyes. He took hold of Mr Crotty by the hands and held him until they were separated. Mr Crotty, the colonel states, had a diamond ring on his finger at the time and in the fracas he received a cut under the right eye.

Both parties took out summonses against the other, leading to a court appearance three days later. To the disappointment of a packed public gallery, the two actors agreed to withdraw the allegations and shake hands, Crotty having alleged that Mapleson was behind a newspaper article that painted him in a bad light.

The Carl Rosa Opera Co. remained in existence until 1960 and was revived in 1997, currently offering a repertoire of Gilbert and Sullivan.

January 20th

1931: A brutal murder took place today in Anfield. It has never been solved, after a guilty verdict was overturned. The *Daily Post and Mercury* reported the following day:

> Liverpool insurance agent William H. Wallace of 29 Wolverton Street, Richmond Park, Anfield, on returning home from business about a quarter to eight last night found his wife Julia lying dead on the floor in the front room with severe wounds in the back of her head. No signs of any struggle were found and no weapon lay near her body. Throughout last night the Liverpool police were searching for an unknown assailant.

A few weeks later William Herbert Wallace was arrested and charged with murder. At his trial, the prosecution alleged Wallace had killed Julia, cleaned himself up and then gone to great lengths to make tram conductors and residents in Allerton – where he had been searching for an address that didn't exist – remember him so his alibi stuck.

He was found guilty and sentenced to death – but for the first time in UK legal history the Court of Appeal overturned the verdict, as it was against the weight of evidence presented.

Wallace died just two years later and was buried in Anfield cemetery alongside Julia. The case has prompted much analysis since, and the true killer is still not known.

January 21st

1953: A bus careered out of control and crashed into a grocer's shop in Kensington. Miraculously, no one was killed.

The 10*d* double-decker service was travelling from Huyton to the city centre at about 10 a.m. when one of its tyres burst. That evening's *Liverpool Echo* reported:

> The driver struggled to keep the bus on the road but within a few yards it collided with a small van parked at the kerbside. The bus careered out of control until it lurched over the pavement and ploughed into the front window of Mr William Davies' grocers' shop on the corner of Kensington and Adelaide Road.

One shop employee was up a ladder when he saw the bus approaching but managed to jump away to safety. The way the *Echo* described the scene, it was as if a bomb had gone off there: 'The bus crashed into the window scattering bricks, glass and tins of groceries over a wide area. The front of the shop from top to bottom was sliced off.'

With the bus leaning at an angle of 45 degrees, another was parked alongside it to stop it crashing over. Of the thirty-two people injured, one took an hour to be cut free by firemen and six were detained at hospital.

January 22nd

1927: A man on this day engaged in what would now be seen as a shocking act of public animal cruelty so that he could continue his tram journey.

It was a Saturday night and the man got on a tram bound for Knotty Ash carrying a basket. He paid his 2*d* fare, but was then asked to get off by the conductor after quacking sounds made it apparent he was carrying ducks. The man refused to move despite an inspector arriving and telling him that the carriage of livestock wasn't allowed under the bylaws.

A policeman was then called, and was about to remove him from the tram when, as the *Daily Post* reported:

A sudden flash of genius saved the situation for him. He quietly put his hands under the lid of the basket. One faint flutter was heard, then another, as the necks of the poor birds were wrung. 'And now where's your livestock?' said he triumphantly. The passengers chuckled, the inspector and policeman descended crestfallen and the car continued on its way.

JANUARY 23RD

1909: Today the RMS *Mauretania* sailed from Liverpool following a refit that saw her given new propellers, enabling an attempt on the trans-Atlantic crossing record.

The ship had only been in service since November 1907, but after two propeller blades were damaged when the ship hit a submerged object in May 1908, Cunard decided to replace both inner shafts with four bladed propellers.

That evening's *Liverpool Echo* reported:

> The quadruple screw liner *Mauretania* sails from Liverpool this afternoon after a period of inactivity during which she has been subject to an extensive overhaul. The *Mauretania* is commanded by Captain Pritchard who was recently appointed Commodore of the Cunard fleet, a well and favourably known commander. Among the passengers on board today are Lord and Lady Atherton, Lady Dorothy Onslow, General Sir H. Rawlinson and numerous others.

By the end of the year the ship had captured both eastbound and westbound records for crossings, with neither being broken for another twenty years. The ship remained in service until 1934 when it was sold for dismantling, having sailed out of Southampton after the First World War.

JANUARY 24TH

1885: Edge Hill Teacher Training College opened. The institution was eventually to become Edge Hill University in Ormskirk.

The college was set up by a group of philanthropists for women only and was non-denominational, the first of its kind in England. Forty-one trainees were enrolled on opening, with Sarah Jane Yelf being the principal. The aim was to produce a 'superior class of elementary school mistresses'.

An event was held at St George's Hall to celebrate the opening, with the *Liverpool Mercury* on 26 January being very enthusiastic: 'It must be gratifying to this community to know that it is the first institution of the kind which has been established to supply trained female teachers to the general market of the country. With such a college in our midst therefore the educational equipment of Liverpool may be regarded as complete and as setting an example to others.'

By 1905 trainee numbers had tripled and the building had been extended. In 1925 the college came under the control of Lancashire Council who built new premises in Ormskirk, which opened in 1933. Since then it has gradually extended, gaining university status in 2006 and having 8,000 full time students in 2011.

JANUARY 25TH

1892: A Special General Meeting (SGM) of Everton Football Club ensured that football in Liverpool would never be the same again. Had members not carried the motions put forward, Everton would have remained at Anfield and there would have been no Liverpool FC.

A dispute had been simmering for some time within the Everton board, with owner of Anfield John Houlding pushing for the club to buy the ground. As this would net him a profit, the other directors did not like the idea; in retaliation, Houlding set a rental rate that they saw as unacceptable.

At the SGM in Liverpool College in Shaw Street, attended by 500 members, four motions were carried. Two of them related to the club becoming a limited company, but the other two were in respect of a move. The Everton Minutes Books record that: 'We offer Mr Houlding £180 per annum for the ground. The Goodison Road site to be selected by the committee in case Mr Houlding does not accept the above offer.'

As expected, Houlding did not accept Everton's offer, the club moved to Goodison and Liverpool FC was formed by Houlding to play in the empty ground he was left with.

JANUARY 26TH

1856: An inquest was held into the unexplained death of Captain Henry Webb, who was found dead aboard his ship the previous day when it berthed in Huskisson Dock.

It was feared that Webb may have taken poison, as he was liable for damages to another vessel that he had been in collision with some months before. The *Liverpool Mercury* reported that Webb's twelve-year-old son told the inquest:

> On Thursday morning he said he felt himself very bad and wished to get out of the world. He gave me charge of his papers and money and told me to take care of myself. He said to the second mate, 'take care of the ship and see that nothing goes out of it, I am going to die'. I woke up yesterday morning about half past five and went to the bed of the deceased, called him but he did not answer. I felt his hand and it was very cold and saw that he was dead.

The inquest jury returned a verdict that Webb had died from taking a narcotic poison, censuring the ship's surgeon for apparent neglect of the condition.

JANUARY 27TH

1934: Liverpool FC met Wirral's Tranmere Rovers in an FA Cup tie at Anfield that attracted what was then a record crowd of 61,036 to the ground. Tranmere were actually drawn to play at home but interest in the tie was so great that for safety reasons it was switched to Anfield.

Despite the teams being two divisions apart, the *Daily Post and Mercury* felt the cup could be a great leveller, commenting on the morning of the match: 'In a match of this sort the element of surprise seems to linger. I feel certain that Liverpool will not have it all their own way.'

The paper was right: Tranmere equalised after a Reds' opener and although it was 2-1 to Liverpool at half time, they didn't add a third until the closing stages. The huge crowd caused chaotic scenes as many fans had to be helped from the overcrowded terracing, with 'Stork' in the following Monday's *Post & Mercury* saying: 'I have never seen such scenes at Anfield, even for an Everton-Liverpool meeting.'

The crowd remained a record attendance at Anfield until 61,905 squeezed in for an FA Cup tie against Wolverhampton Wanderers in 1952.

JANUARY 28TH

1896: Liverpool's newsvendors were given a special treat at St George's Hall to allow them some respite from the hardships they generally faced. The newsboys and girls tended to come from the poorest families and in many cases had no homes to return to at night. They did not work for the papers, but instead purchased copies at a discounted rate and sold them at normal price. Crucially, they could not return any unsold copies for refund, meaning they could be seen and heard from morning until late at night in all major roads of the city.

The occasion at St George's Hall was paid for out of the proceeds of a football match between paper employees and railway workers, as well as generous donations from local businesses.

The following day's *Liverpool Daily Courier* reported:

> The occasion was an exceptional one. These children had not only souls to be saved but bodies to be cared for. The doors were opened at seven o'clock and in a few moments there was a stampede into the hall. More than 2,000 were admitted, each presented with an orange and an apple and a bag containing such tasty articles as a bunloaf, mince pie and meat pie.

After listening to some complimentary speeches there was a concert in which they participated in the singing.

JANUARY 29TH

1872: Over 100 men appeared in the Liverpool Police Court charged with drink related offences from over the weekend. The following day's *Liverpool Mercury* welcomed new initiatives that meant numbers were reducing. Under the headline 'THE DRUNKARDS LIST', the paper commented:

> There was an improvement slight it is true, but still an improvement in the state of affairs at the police court yesterday morning. The drunk and disorderly cases which the previous Monday numbered 130 now only reached 115; and as a few months ago before inebriates were threatened with exposure as well as heavy penalties it was common enough to hear nearly 200 drunken cases brought before the bench every Monday morning. It may be reasonably inferred that some good has resulted from the severe measures adopted.

In an attempt to deter drunkenness, authorities had recently begun offering those brought before the courts a straight choice of a fine or imprisonment and also publishing names of employers. Some employers had been unhappy about these details being made public, but the *Mercury* took a different view commenting: 'They will be gainers if the sobriety and steadiness of their employees be increased.'

JANUARY 30TH

1970: There was an unusual police chase in Fairfield when a bullock made a run for it from Stanley Abattoir. The story made the front page of that evening's *Liverpool Echo*, which reported: 'Ferdinand the bullock broke away from the Stanley Abattoir in Prescot Road and escaped into the lush pasture of nearby Newsham Park. Three policemen in two panda cars raced to the scene but as every cowboy knows it is easier to rustle on a horse.'

The bullock eventually got a bit too sure of himself, heading out of the park. As the *Echo* report went on: 'Ferdinand too must have realised they were at a disadvantage for he trotted off with confidence to the park exit and Sheil Road. But as he turned into Kensington with the panda cars at his heels it was clear that the rodeo was almost over. Ferdinand was finally surrounded in the backyard of a television shop and taken back to the abattoir.'

JANUARY 31ST

1916: Liverpool had a lucky escape when the pilot of a German Zeppelin airship failed to navigate properly.

Nine airships left their bases at Freidrichshafen and Lowenthal with the orders to cross England and bomb Liverpool, showing the British government that Germans were not limited to bombing southern and eastern coastal areas. However, with radar yet to be invented and a cloudy sky, the pilots had to use time calculations and gaps in the cloud to judge where they were. Captain Max Dietrich, having thought he had just passed Manchester, homed in on 'Liverpool' – but in fact he had passed over Derby and bombed Tipton, Bradley, Wednesbury and Walsall instead.

Thirty-five people were killed in the bombings, including the Mayor of Walsall and three children in one family in Wednesbury. The next evening's *Liverpool Echo* published a considerably limited statement by the War Office which said: 'A raid by six or seven airships took place last night, a number of bombs were dropped but no considerable damage reported.'

Captain Dietrich was killed the following November when his airship was shot down after a raid over Hartlepool. Twenty-five years later German bombers did find their way to Liverpool, leading to devastating consequences.

FEBRUARY 1ST

1879: A strike broke out amongst 20,000 stevedores and labourers on the docks over cuts in pay. The Liverpool Shipowner's Association reduced pay by *6d* a day, an 11 per cent cut. They said the move was necessary due to a reduced amount of freight coming through the port.

The *Liverpool Mercury* was not too sympathetic about the dockers' plight, commenting on 3 February:

> Groups of idle men could be seen lounging about the docks of Liverpool and Birkenhead. Even those who assisted them on a former occasion to procure an increase stand aloof from this movement which under the circumstances they regard as little less than suicidal. A reduction of 6d per day has just come into effect as regard the wages of corn porters, weighers etc.

The *Mercury* predicted that the strike would peter out within a few days – but they were wrong. It went on for over two weeks, with more workers joining in. Eventually a compromise was reached where the dockers returned to work on the reduced rate but with increased overtime payments.

FEBRUARY 2ND

1955: There was an interesting debate in the Liverpool Council chamber when members narrowly voted to close a barber's shop in the Corporation Transport Works in Edge Lane.

The barber's shop had been there since the Second World War and allowed workers to get a haircut during office hours. However, the transport committee argued this was no longer relevant and the barbers' room was needed for expansion. The resident barber was a sixty-five-year-old man who worked on a self-employed basis. The National Hairdressers Federation had complained about the special treatment he received in not having to pay for electric and heating.

After the transport committee, chaired by Alderman W.G. Gregson, recommended closure, Labour's Councillor Cain urged that the motion be postponed by three years until the time when the barber could draw a pension. The following day the *Daily Post* reported that Labour leader John Braddock, husband of MP Bessie, said: 'Think carefully before you vote a man of 65 out of a job'.

In the end the transport committee just about got their way, winning by sixty-five votes to sixty, their cause helped by after an overnight dash by two councillors whose return from a civic visit to Madeira was delayed by bad weather.

February 3rd

1868: Tragedy struck on the River Mersey when the Liverpool River Police boat capsized, leading to the loss of one officer, Constable Henry Madden.

The river police had been in existence since 1865, funded by the Mersey Docks & Harbour Co. but with its officers being sworn in as borough police constables. The boat was undergoing a routine patrol of the river between Rock Ferry and Tranmere when weather conditions took a turn for the worse. The following day's *Daily Post* reported: 'Yesterday morning a lamentable accident occurred to the river police boat *Clint*. The wind got up and though it lasted for but a short time it resulted in a most serious calamity on the river. The sail, which was brailed up was caught by a sudden squall, the little craft was turned completely over.'

Two lifeboats exercising off Rock Ferry raced to the scene and managed to save five of the crew, but Madden had already drowned. Had the lifeboats not been where they were, all six men may well have been lost.

At the subsequent inquest, the coroner recommended that the design of the boat, which allowed it to sit too deep in the water, played a part in the accident.

FEBRUARY 4TH

1893: The Liverpool Overhead Railway opened. The 6-mile line ran from Alexandra Dock in Bootle to Herculaneum Dock in Toxteth. Later extensions were made to Dingle in the south and Seaforth in the north, connecting with the Lancashire & Yorkshire Railway.

Two days later the *Liverpool Mercury* reported:

Liverpool is the first city in England to build an overhead railway, and the first in the world to adopt electricity as a means of working such a railway. On Saturday, the formality of opening this unique undertaking was performed by the Marquis of Salisbury. All vessels in the dock and surrounding streets were bedecked with bunting, and the scene was of the gayest description, as equipages and cabs, the picturesque uniforms of the mounted police, the general animation, the large bodies of police under their inspectors lent no small affect to the ensemble. Speeches were made and the presentation of a small silver inkstand was made to Lord Salisbury, who started the electric current of 2,000 horse power which magically draws trains over the lines. When the ceremony was over the party accompanied Lord Salisbury to Sandon Station where a specially decorated train was waiting to convey them on the first official trip on the line.

The railway was in use for sixty-three years.

February 5th

1914: George Ball was sentenced to death after murdering his employer and dumping her body in the Leeds and Liverpool canal.

Ball worked in a tarpaulin shop in Old Hall Street, and on 10 December 1913 he sexually assaulted Christina Bradfield and battered her to death. He then put her body in a sack and pushed it in a handcart to the canal, bullying another shop assistant, Samuel Elltoft, into helping him. The following day the body was discovered. Elltoft was arrested almost immediately, but Ball managed to stay on the run for a week. The *Liverpool Echo* dubbed it the 'sack murder trial', and on 5 February, the final day, the handcart was brought to court. It reported that evening: 'Shortly before ten o'clock the curious strained their necks as they saw two detectives bringing along the handcart upon which Miss Bradfield's mutilated body had been.'

Around 4,000 people had waited on the plateau outside St George's Hall to hear the verdict. Elltoft received four years' imprisonment for being an accessory after the fact. The next day's *Daily Post* was damning in its assessment of Ball, stating: 'No tears need be wasted over Miss Bradfield's murderer. George Ball was guilty of a cruel and heartless murder.'

FEBRUARY 6TH

1959: Four prisoners formed a human ladder to make a run for it from Walton Gaol.

The men had arrived at the gaol on remand after being charged with house breaking. At 6.30 p.m. they were left alone in the reception area for a few minutes and formed the chain to escape through a skylight. The next morning's *Daily Post* reported: 'Two of the men were caught in the prison grounds but the others scaled the 32 foot wall fronting on Hornby Road and dropped to the ground outside, almost at the feet of a warder going off duty. There was a struggle but the men managed to escape.'

One of the men was picked up at a flat in Upper Frederick Street that night but the other remained at large until the next morning. He was caught at Edge Lane after being chased from Tunnel Road where a policeman going off duty had seen him getting off a bus.

FEBRUARY 7TH

1947: The Government announced a daytime electrical shut down except for 'essential services' as the cold weather continued to bite, to the consternation of Liverpool housewives.

The measures were announced by Minister of Fuel Manny Shinwell, with electric supply to be cut off from nine o'clock to twelve o'clock in the morning and two o'clock to four o'clock in the afternoon due to a fuel crisis caused by the country having been under a blanket of snow since 21 January.

The following day's *Daily Post* reported that many Merseyside housewives, who relied on electricity for cooking a midday meal for their families, were completely perplexed at the situation. The paper told how Mrs M.A. Mylchreest, Honorary Secretary of the British Housewives League, had sent a telegram to Shinwell, saying: 'Please state how housewives can cook midday meals, tend for the sick and care for infants in all electric homes without supply. Are you devoid of common sense?'

The month went on to become the coldest February on record and restrictions on electricity use remained until April.

FEBRUARY 8TH

1996: The Most Reverend Derek Worlock, Archbishop of Liverpool, died after a long battle with lung cancer.

Born in London in 1920, he was ordained as a priest in 1944 and was Bishop of Portsmouth before coming to Liverpool in 1976. He worked with Anglican Bishop David Sheppard for the good of the city, which was faced with growing unemployment, the Toxteth Riots, Heysel and Hillsborough during their reigns. They wrote two books, *Better Together* and *With Hope in Our Hearts*.

His obituary in the *Independent* the next day paid tribute to the partnership:

> They stood in for each other and sometimes preached joint sermons in which one would complete the thought of the other. Their principle was, 'Do everything together, except the things which conscience forces us to do apart'. In a Liverpool which had the potential to be a British Belfast and in which older people could remember rowdy Orange marches, this was as dramatic as it was novel. Together they found a distinctive Merseyside voice in addressing the social problems of the Thatcher era, of whose individualist ethos they were sharply critical. In Liverpool they kept alive forgotten notions such as common good and community. They refused to believe that the weakest or the unemployed should go to the wall.

FEBRUARY 9TH

1961: The Beatles performed in the Cavern Club for the first time. Although John Lennon and Paul McCartney had played there in 1958 when they were still known as The Quarrymen, this was the first performance at the club under the name of The Beatles, and George Harrison's first appearance. The Beatles already had quite a following in Liverpool and were now returning after three months in Hamburg, where their stamina and repertoire had improved considerably. Harrison very nearly didn't make the performance for the unadvertised concert, being at first refused entry due to the strict dress code that forbade jeans.

In Spencer Leigh's book *The Cavern*, the club's manager Ray McFall recalled: 'They were different and they were very well rehearsed because they had come back from three months of torture in Hamburg. The other groups were like Cliff Richard and the Shadows, but The Beatles' music was so vibrant...'

Word soon got around and their lunchtime sessions became extremely popular, leading to local record shop owner Brian Epstein to drop in, become their manager and secure a recording deal. Over the next two and a half years The Beatles played the venue 292 times.

FEBRUARY 10TH

1898: Two underwear thieves who worked on the railways were sentenced at Liverpool Police Court. The following day's *Liverpool Mercury* reported: 'James Gaffney and John Henry Jones, who were shunters for the Cheshire Lines committee and of respectable appearance, pleaded guilty to having purloined a quantity of underclothing from a parcel at Huskisson station which had been consigned from London to Dublin.'

Jones was also convicted of stealing boots along with Robert Pye and Walter Hughes. The *Mercury* said that they: 'Admitted having stolen thirteen pairs of boots from a parcel that had been consigned to the company for conveyance from Leicester to Southport. The larceny was committed at the Walton sidings.'

The four men were all given fines ranging from £4 1s to £10 14s. They were given the opportunity to arrange monthly payments but warned they faced imprisonment if they weren't met.

FEBRUARY 11TH

1810: Disaster struck when twenty-five children were killed following the collapse of a spire in the church of St Nicholas on the waterfront.

Worshippers were gathering for a Sunday morning service at the time. As the bells were rung, part of the steeple gave way, causing the spire to collapse – just as girls from the local Moorfields charity school were walking down the aisle.

In 1863 an eye-witness account was published in James Stonehouse's *Recollections of Old Liverpool*:

> The spire fell with a frightful and appalling crash into the body of the building. Amidst the rising dust were heard the dreadful screams of the poor children who had become involved in the ruins. Twenty-eight little ones were at length brought out, of whom twenty-three were dead; five were alive, and were taken to the Infirmary, but of these, only three survived. They were horribly maimed, and so disfigured that they were scarcely recognizable. Of all the pitiable sights I ever beheld, the sight of these little things laid on the grass was the most piteous; and, as, one by one they were claimed and taken away.

The cause of the accident was believed to have been the spire, which had been added in 1756; it had not been placed correctly on the old tower. This, added to the ringing of bells and weather erosion, led to its eventual collapse.

FEBRUARY 12TH

1963: Two *Coronation Street* actors were surprised to end up on a Liverpool stage after rehearsing all day in Manchester.

Kenneth Cope, who played Jed Stone, and Christine Hargreaves, who played Elsie Tanner's lodger Christine Appleby, were persuaded by student David Thomas to come to Liverpool and go on stage at the Students' Union during a performance of their 'pantopera', a musical pantomime.

The following evening's *Liverpool Echo*, under the headline 'SNATCH OF THE DAY' reported:

> Two television stars were whisked away from a Manchester studio last night and ninety minutes later were making a personal appearance on the stage of the Student's Union. Outside the studio where they were rehearsing they were approached by David Thomas and persuaded to accompany him to Liverpool. Mr Cope, whose parents live in Wavertree, had already planned to visit his parents last night and his wife followed him in another car.

A third television star, Lance Perceval of *That Was The Week That Was*, was also approached but had to decline as he was already booked to appear in cabaret in Manchester.

FEBRUARY 13TH

1889: Liverpool Council agreed to purchase a collection of drawings that had been made by William Herdman.

Born in 1805, Herdman sketched many of Liverpool's buildings creating a fascinating historical portrait of a town that was expanding rapidly. He also copied and improved many earlier works, and he died in 1882. Herdman produced many drawings of Liverpool, Wales and Ireland for Alderman William Bennett. On Bennett's death in 1889, his collection, including almost 1,500 drawings by Herdman, was put up for auction. Liverpool Arts Committee were allowed to bid £300 but they were instead sold to a local dealer for £341. However, Sir James Picton put forward a resolution at the Town Council on 13 February:

> That the collection of drawings, principally by the late W.G. Herdman, 943 in number, illustrative of the history and architecture of Liverpool, collected by the late Alderman William Bennett, now offered to the Council, be purchased for the sum of £450 out of monies raised by the Rate for 1889 laid under the Liverpool Library & Museum Act, 1852.

The motion was carried by thirty-two votes to six, giving the library and museum some of Herdman's best work, and leaving a local dealer with a tidy profit.

FEBRUARY 14TH

1996: Former Liverpool FC manager Bob Paisley died after a long battle against Alzheimer's disease.

Born in the Durham village of Hetton-le-Hole in 1919, Paisley joined Liverpool in 1939 but had to wait until 1946 to make his debut due to the Second World War. As a midfielder he won the league title in 1947, but it was as a manager where he became a legend, guiding the club to six league championships, three European Cups, three League Cups and a UEFA Cup in just nine years in charge. Despite such glories, he remained a humble man and liked nothing more than to be at home watching television with his wife and playing with his grandchildren.

He died at 9.30 a.m. in Arncliffe Court nursing home, Halewood. That night's *Liverpool Echo* wrote:

> Wife Jessie was at his bedside and his sons, Graham and Robert, arrived shortly after he died. He spent the last fourteen months at the nursing home where he and his family had become very popular. Mr Paisley OBE devoted his working life to Liverpool FC. and became the country's most successful manager during his nine years at the helm.

Paisley was buried in the graveyard of St Peter's church in Woolton. His gravestone says: 'He remained an ordinary man amidst extraordinary achievements.'

FEBRUARY 15TH

1971: Liverpool got to grips with Decimalisation, with the process going relatively smoothly.

The public had been getting prepared for Decimalisation with the 5p, 10p and 50p coins having already been introduced and both sets of prices shown. But this was the day when the 1p and 2p coins would be introduced to complete the transition, and prices had to be displayed in the decimal format first and foremost (rather than in £/s/d).

That night's *Liverpool Echo*, now costing 3p as opposed to 7*d*, reported that there were no major problems: 'The D-day switchover on Merseyside went smoothly today although there were reports of an initial slowdown in money changing as was anticipated. Generally shoppers and commuters took a little bit longer over transactions but cashiers, shop assistants and booking clerks, already trained to deal with decimalisation, were eager to help'.

An *Echo* reporter wrote after shopping in Church Street:

The first few hours has proved practically painless. The smoothness of the transaction is down to two factors – the good humoured acceptance of the public and even more, the patience of shop employees. Although the shops are accepting £/s/d all change is being given in decimal currency and assistants everywhere have been slowly counting out the change.

FEBRUARY 16TH

1894: There was an unusual charity football match at Goodison Park. Everton's 'A' team took on a team of actors playing in pantomime in Liverpool and Manchester, with proceeds raised going to victims of the Santander dynamite explosion in Spain. This had occurred the previous November, when a steamship, carrying dynamite, exploded in Santander harbour, killing 500 and injuring 2,000 more.

The following day's *Liverpool Mercury* reported: 'A large company assembled who were rewarded by a most humorous and entertaining display of football, the proceeds of which it is hoped will help materially towards the good object for which the match was set up.'

Ladies from the theatres sold refreshments, cigars and flowers to raise more funds, the *Mercury* commenting that: 'Their bewitching smiles and entertaining conversation had much to do with the ultimate proceeds of the match.'

Everton played in their traditional blue strip, while the actors wore theatrical dress, with one as a schoolboy and another as Mrs Sinbad. Despite the unusual kit, the actors ran out 4-1 winners and after the game the ladies took part in a 50-yard race.

FEBRUARY 17TH

1932: Liverpool housewives were promised that housework would soon be a 'scientific delight'.

The Electrical Association for Women (Liverpool branch) were holding their annual meeting at the Town Hall. Lord Mayor Alderman J.C. Cross and Caroline Haslett, Director of the Women's Engineering Society, were in attendance. The following day's *Daily Post and Mercury* reported that Alderman Cross told those present that the city will be a cleaner place thanks to electricity as there will be less air-polluting chimneys. Haslett said as she took the stand: 'Electricity is going to make housework a scientific delight but it is essential that women should learn how to get the best use out of electrical appliances.'

Haslett made it clear that the public need educating over electricity, pointing to an example of an old lady who had recently written to the society asking for somebody to go and demonstrate a vacuum cleaner to her, but to also take some electricity as she was not connected. She also predicted that there would be career opportunities for women as demonstrators and that: 'All housecraft in future will be electrical and electricity is not just a passing fashion.'

February 18th

1895: A brutal murder took place in Redcross Street when an elderly man was battered to death.

Edward Moyse shared his home with fifteen-year-old John Needham who did chores for him. That night, his ex-lodger William Miller returned after being away at sea and was allowed to stay, only to set about Moyse and Needham with a poker whilst they were sleeping. Under the headline 'SHOCKING TRAGEDY IN LIVERPOOL – OLD MAN BRUTALLY MURDERED' the *Liverpool Mercury* reported on 20 February:

> Early yesterday morning information conveyed to Liverpool police of a murder committed in the heart of the city under a circumstance of the most horrible and mysterious character. The victim is an old man Edward Moyse who eked out a humble living by selling bibles from a stall at the south end of George's Dock. The old man was known as a quiet, inoffensive and respectful individual. The boy Needham remains at the Northern Hospital in a critical condition. He suffered no less than fourteen wounds about the head. An operation was performed on him, the results of which appear satisfactory.

Needham was able to give a description to police, leading to an ID parade at his hospital bedside at which he picked Miller out (thanks, in part, to a nervous twitch he had). Miller was later hanged for the murder at Walton gaol.

FEBRUARY 19TH

1963: Runcorn was confirmed as the location of a new dormitory town for Liverpool to house people being moved out of slum-clearance areas.

The *Liverpool Echo* that evening reported that the town's population would almost triple from 26,000 to 70,000 and had been selected due to its good transport links. Some industry would be developed but many workers were envisaged as commuting to Liverpool.

The *Echo* stated that although there had been objections, Liverpool's need to clear its slum areas was more pressing:

> Runcorn was first mentioned as a possible dormitory six years ago but there were agricultural objections. It is now felt that Liverpool's pressing need for land overcomes these. Orders designating the site will be drafted and advertised and there will be opportunity for objections and if necessary public inquiries. When the project takes final shape the development will proceed under the Town Development Act. It has been accepted that if Liverpool is to clear its slums, homes will need to be made available elsewhere for the displaced people to live in. This is what is planned for Runcorn.

The development gathered particular pace in the 1970s and Runcorn's population is now around 60,000.

FEBRUARY 20TH

1946: A fire at Kirkdale's Canada Number 2 Dock endangered ships and destroyed a dock shed. The following day's *Daily Post* reported:

> The fire was seen in the corner of the dock shed by a dock labourer a few minutes before three o'clock. In less than five minutes an emergency fire engine had arrived from the dock fire station nearby but the gale had whipped the flames into a fierce blaze which had become unmanageable. Forty dockers were loading sisal hemp into the Swedish steamer *Halmstad* alongside the warehouse and they were cut off when the flames destroyed the gangway. Two tugs were fortunately at hand in the dock and at once hauled the steamer out of reach of the flames.

It took an hour to bring the fire under control after a fire boat attacked the flames from the water and considerable damage was caused. The *Post* continued: 'It was impossible to save the shed and the bales of hemp and efforts were concentrated on preventing the fire from spreading to the Canada graving dock, pumping station and Cunard White Star liner *Samaria* which was lying in the graving dock.'

The fire was described by the following day's edition as the worst in the docks since the Blitz of 1941. Four firemen were injured, including one blown into the water by a gale, and hundreds of pigeons were trapped and killed.

FEBRUARY 21ST

1931: Margaret Beavan, Liverpool's first female Lord Mayor, died of pneumonia.

Known as the Little Mother of Liverpool – and, less complimentarily, 'the Clever Beggar' – she was a tireless campaigner for child welfare. She was a driving force behind the setting up of the Leasowe Open Air Hospital, which provided post-hospital care for children, and the Child Welfare Association, which sent sick children to the countryside to convalesce. In 1924 she was elected to Liverpool Council, representing Prince's Park, and became Lord Mayor in 1927. She also served as a magistrate.

On 23 February the *Liverpool Echo* reported Stipendiary Magistrate Stuart Deacon's tribute to her that day: 'She has blazed a trail and the torch she has left behind will be carried by others in years to come'.

Lord Mayor Edwin Thompson made the following tribute: 'A great character has joined the ages. To only a few is given the ability to leave behind such a mark as she has done. She has died many, many years before her time but her work will be remembered for all time.'

Her memory lived on in the Margaret Beavan Special School in West Derby, which closed in 2004.

FEBRUARY 22ND

1957: The annual report of the Bootle Borough Police was published, in which the Chief Constable H.G. Legg blamed lenient magistrates for a rise in crime.

That evening's *Liverpool Echo* reported that there had been 1,437 indictable crimes in 1957, compared to 1,191 in 1956. The report was quite clear about the reasons, saying:

> Statistics do show the Bootle bench is one of the most lenient in the country and there is reason to believe that some criminals are taking advantage of this leniency. These people weigh up the risk of their criminal acts and are apprehensive of being dealt with by one court while being light-hearted about another.

However, Legg was happy with one aspect of sentencing: 'One feature in our local court I feel most commendable is the almost invariable practice of ordering compensation to the victim, a matter frequently overlooked by superior courts.'

Somewhat surprisingly, he was particularly bothered about child cyclists who he felt were either a danger to pedestrians or themselves if they didn't know road safety: 'I appeal to parents to face up to responsibilities and get away from the idea that because the child next door has a bicycle theirs must have one too.'

FEBRUARY 23RD

1959: Health authorities in Liverpool began an onslaught on tuberculosis (TB), taking steps that they hoped would eradicate the disease in the city within a few years.

That evening's *Liverpool Echo* reported: 'Today all the might of medical administration has started to move into action in Liverpool in the largest action against TB ever taken in this country.' The measures included screening machines in many locations, including city-centre stores, guaranteed hospital beds for anyone in the early stages of the disease and home helps offering domestic assistance and cleaning services to reduce the risk of the disease spreading. Extra milk and childcare was also on offer for those being treated at home. As part of the publicity campaign, Dr Clifford Martin, Bishop of Liverpool, was pictured next to the slogan, 'I've been x-rayed. Have you?'

The following day the *Echo* reported that officials were satisfied with the beginning of the campaign. A reported 19,173 residents were x-rayed, less than the 20,000 hoped for but still a good number given that seven machines broke down.

FEBRUARY 24TH

1935: Reverend James Hamilton, former minister of Liverpool Presbyterian church, died in a nursing home at the age of seventy-five.

Originally from Linlithgow, he was first an assistant minister in Kinnoull, Perthshire before coming to Liverpool in 1889 to become minister at St Andrew's in Rodney Street, which had been built for the local Scottish Presbyterian population in 1823. He brought stability to the church and during his long spell as minister he also held the prestigious position of president of the Athenaeum Club from 1926 to 1927.

The following day's *Evening Express* paid tribute by saying: 'Mr Hamilton in his 46 years ministerial service built up a numerically strong and enthusiastic scholarship. He was chaplain for many years to the Liverpool Scottish. Mr Hamilton leaves a widow, a son and a daughter.'

Hamilton was succeeded as minister by James Douglas, who died after just two years in the role.

FEBRUARY 25TH

1905: The Cunard liner *Caronia* made its maiden voyage from Liverpool. Built on the River Clyde, she could carry 1,500 passengers and weighed over 19,000 tons, making her the largest ship in the Cunard fleet, along with her sister ship *Carmania*. She sailed for New York at 4.30 p.m. on a Saturday afternoon, the *Liverpool Daily Courier* reporting on the 27 February:

> Crowds gathered in the vicinity had an opportunity of forming some conception of her enormous hulk. She commenced to glide away from her berth promptly on the advertisement time. As she got on the move the barriers to the landing stage were removed and the crowds of people rushed to get a nearer view of the great ship. Between them and the passengers there was an exchange of farewell greetings by means of pocket handkerchiefs. Hundreds were waved aloft and 'bon voyage' was wished through the medium of cheers.

She operated the Liverpool to New York route until the First World War when she was requisitioned as a troop ship. After the war she sailed from Liverpool to Boston, Halifax, New York and Quebec before being scrapped in 1932.

FEBRUARY 26TH

1839: The first Grand National took place. Billed as the Grand Liverpool Steeplechase, it was run over two circuits of Aintree racecourse, with twenty fences (including a stone wall).

Seventeen horses took part in the race, which was won by a horse named Lottery, ridden by Jem Mason. At the sixth fence, Captain Martin Becher came off his horse and was catapulted over the fence, seeking shelter in the brook on the other side. This led to the naming of the fence: Becher's Brook.

Despite an attendance of 40,000, the *Liverpool Mercury* was not so enthusiastic, writing the next day: 'We have heard with alarm and regret that it is in contemplation to establish steeplechasing annually or periodically in this neighbourhood. If any such design is seriously entertained we trust that some means will be adopted to defeat it!'

No such means proposed by the *Mercury* were adopted: the race became known as the Grand National from 1847 and is now watched by half a billion people in over one hundred countries around the world.

FEBRUARY 27TH

1937: A tablet in memory of former manager and chairman John McKenna was unveiled at Anfield by Liverpool FC.

McKenna played a huge part in the development of the club, persuading the Board to make the move from the Lancashire League to the Football League in 1893 and recruiting a number of Scottish players that gained promotion to the 1st Division at the first attempt. He then persuaded ex-Sunderland manager Tom Watson to come to Liverpool in 1896, a move that led to two league title successes.

McKenna became president of the Football League in 1910, holding the position until his death in 1936 at the age of eighty-one.

The memorial was unveiled by Will Cuff, chairman of Everton and vice president of the Football League, before a match between Liverpool and Brentford that was drawn 2-2. That evening's *Liverpool Echo* reported:

A memorial tablet to the late Mr John McKenna, former president of the Football League, vice president of the Football Association and chairman of Liverpool FC who died last year was unveiled at Liverpool FC's ground today by Mr W.C. Cuff, chairman of Everton FC and vice president of the Football League, who said Mr McKenna was a 'football genius'.

FEBRUARY 28TH

1911: There was a fatal accident at Liverpool docks when a construction worker was killed.

The accident took place at Gladstone Dock, which was still under excavation. The following day's *Liverpool Daily Courier* reported:

An alarming incident unfortunately attended by loss of life occurred yesterday at the new Gladstone Dock. At about nine o'clock the sand and soil were being lifted into buckets by means of a crane, emptied into trucks and carried away. The huge bucket which lifts about a ton of weight at a time was in mid-air when something snapped and the bucket with its enormous load fell back into the excavation. As it descended the bucket struck one of the workmen, James McGuiness of Adenside Street, Bootle, who was killed outright and four other men were slightly injured but after being attended to at Bootle Hospital they were allowed to go home.

FEBRUARY 29TH

1836: Liverpool Borough Police Force commenced operational duty. There were already three police groups in the city – night watch, day police and dock police. The Reform Act of 1832 allowed for the creation of a borough force, leading to the amalgamation of the night and day police, with a number of further new officers recruited. The dock police were absorbed into the new force a year later.

The first head constable was Michael Whitty, former superintendent of the night watch. On 4 March the *Liverpool Mercury* welcomed the move and called for further measures, saying:

> We doubt not that we shall now for the first time have the benefit of an efficient day and night police force. We allude to the difficulty experienced frequently in finding a policeman at the precise moment his services are required. The difficulty might be alleviated by requiring every constable, when off duty, to affix to the door of his dwelling house a notice of his being employed in the police force, by which means the public would at all times know where to apply for assistance. This plan has been adopted by the municipal authorities in Bath.

When Whitty left his post of head constable in 1847 he founded the *Daily Post*, which at 1*d* was cheaper than the *Mercury*.

MARCH 1ST

1971: As The Beatles were in the High Court dissolving their partnership, there were frantic scenes at the Liverpool Empire as thousands queued for tickets to see the Rolling Stones.

Tickets for two concerts which were to take place on the same day went on sale on a Monday morning with some fans having queued since the Saturday night. Around 100 police had to be called in to keep order, with the next day's *Daily Post* reporting:

> When the doors of the theatre opened the head of the queue waiting in Coal Street suddenly surged forward. Immediately a call went out to all divisions of the Liverpool and Bootle Police. With fans crowding the doors and spilling onto the pavement, police set to work relieving the pressure from behind by thinning out the crowd. Later, police horses were called in to help with crowd control.

The police had everything in control by the afternoon and no arrests were made. The Empire's manager Terry Jones told the *Post*: 'In all my years connected with the theatre I've never seen anything like it. In eight hours we sold all of the 5,100 tickets.'

Although the Rolling Stones continue to perform today, they have not played in Liverpool since 1971.

MARCH 2ND

1871: The *Oceanic* sailed from Liverpool for her maiden voyage but she later caused embarrassment to officials when she broke down and had to turn back around.

Powered by a combination of steam and sail, the White Star liner provided a major step forward in passenger comfort, with running water in most of the first-class cabins and larger portholes to allow more light. In steerage class, single passengers were segregated from families.

The *Liverpool Daily Courier* reported on her maiden voyage the following day:

> Yesterday evening just a little before six o'clock the new screw steamer *Oceanic*, the pioneer of a new steam line between Liverpool and New York, sailed from the Mersey. This vessel by her outline and uncommon rig has created an immense sensation amongst nautical connoisseurs. The *Oceanic* had on board a full cargo and fair complement of passengers from both classes.

Unfortunately a metal bearing on the vessel fused off the coast of Ireland and she was forced to turn back and dock at Holyhead for repairs before continuing the voyage. The *Oceanic* went on to overcome this early setback and was a commercial success for the White Star Line, breaking speed records on the Liverpool-Hong Kong and Yokohama-San Francisco routes.

MARCH 3RD

1884: Two sisters were hanged after killing members of their own family to claim life insurance money.

Irish widows Catherine Flannagan and Margaret Higgins lived in Vauxhall and poisoned Flannagan's son John, along with Mary Jennings and Margaret Higgins (the daughters of two lodgers) and finally Margaret's second husband Thomas. It was Thomas's death that led to the police investigation after his brother found out that his life had been insured with a number of companies beforehand. Arsenic was found in his corpse, and also in the bodies of the other three victims when they were exhumed.

Both sisters were found guilty of murder, the jury taking just twenty minutes to reach a verdict. They were executed together on a snowy morning at Kirkdale Gaol, the following day's *Liverpool Mercury* reporting:

> Despite the inclement state of the weather a crowd began to assemble outside the wall of the prison. By eight o'clock the crowd numbered fully a thousand, nearly all of whom were of the lower class, whose morbid curiosity made them utterly reckless of the sleet and wind. Both women wore an appearance of resignation. They vainly attempted to utter responses to Father Bonte's prayers. During the fearful ordeal they never looked at one another. At the given signal the bolt was drawn, death being evidently instantaneous.

MARCH 4TH

1954: Liverpool's slum clearance programme gathered further pace when the city's biggest ever housing contract was awarded for development in Kirkby.

The next day's *Daily Post* reported:

> A housing contract more than twice as large as any before in Liverpool history was accepted yesterday by the Liverpool Corporation Housing Committee. Under its terms Unit Construction Company will build 3,511 dwellings and 444 garages on the Kirkby estate for £4,822,510. The tender provides for the completion of all outstanding dwellings in the Southdene neighbourhood, a part of Northwood and practically the entire Westvale neighbourhood.

The contract was more than twice as large as what was awarded for 1,570 Kirkby dwellings in 1952 and allowed for the building of houses, flats, maisonettes and aged persons' flats. The *Post* reported that the Kirkby scheme was gaining nationwide publicity: 'The exceptional rate of progress on the Kirkby estate is attracting national attention. Last year more than 1,000 dwellings were completed. A further 1,500 will be finished there this year.'

Despite the new housing, there were many who didn't want to see their community broken up and move away from the inner city to the new properties, especially as amenities were not being built at the same rate.

MARCH 5TH

1977: On this day boxer John Conteh beat Len Hutchins at Liverpool Stadium to retain the World Light Heavyweight Championship.

Kirkby fighter Conteh had been the WBC Light Heavyweight Champion since 1974 and this was the fourth defence of his title, but the first to be fought in Liverpool. The previous night's *Liverpool Echo* dubbed it 'the biggest night the Stadium has ever known', and reported that 100 extra stewards would be on duty. Thirty-six rugby league players had been drafted in to help with security for the three thousand eight hundred crowd.

Conteh won after a third-round stoppage, Hutchins having received a cut in the first round. On 7 March the *Echo* quoted Conteh as saying: 'I admit I went a bit wild. But when you see a cut like that all you can think about is that the fight is as good as over and the champagne is waiting.'

Conteh's next defence saw him lose the title in Belgrade and he never regained it, losing in two attempts against Matthew Saad Muhammad in Atlantic City. The Liverpool Stadium never hosted another world title fight and closed in 1985.

MARCH 6TH

1940: Liverpool Council agreed to raise tram fares despite strenuous opposition from Labour councillors.

The following day's *Daily Post* reported that Councillor Clegg, who seconded a motion to resist the rise, told the council chamber: 'If workers know that fares are to be increased and the service is not to be improved there is going to be the most unholy row all over the city.'

However, Alderman Shennan of the Conservatives said that the city's population had fallen by 100,000 since war had broken out seven months earlier so losses were inevitable if fares didn't rise. He also refused to consider subsidising fares with the rates, as it was unfair for Liverpool ratepayers to be paying when many users came from outside the city.

Maximum fares rose from 2*d* to 2½*d*, with the *Post* reporting: 'Ultimately after further protests the committee's scheme of fares and stages was adopted by a large majority on a show of hands.'

MARCH 7TH

1939: Liverpool's Licensing Justices refused an application from Ind Coope & Allsop brewery for darts to be allowed in their seventy city pubs. In a strange anomaly, darts was allowed in pubs in every city in the country but remained banned in Liverpool, where billiards was the only game that could be played.

R.K. Milne, representing the brewery, cited that darts would lead to better behaviour, the next day's *Daily Post* reporting him as telling the court: 'There can be no doubt that the playing of the game must lead to increased sobriety. People keen on the game are not likely to take too much intoxicating liquor.'

Milne also claimed that in Cardiff more women were going to pubs as darts was allowed and that pubs should be social places with other things to do, not plain drinking establishments. Despite his pleas the justices rejected the application, the Chair stating: 'In the interests of the licensees carrying out their difficult and responsible duties, the committee does not look upon the application with approval.'

MARCH 8TH

1901: At the Liverpool Police Court, a labourer was sentenced following an assault on a tram passenger who complained about his smoking. The next day's *Daily Post* reported:

Frederick Lunberg, accountant, summonsed Henry Shepherd, labourer for having assaulted him. It appeared from the evidence of the complainant that the parties were both passengers on a Smithdown Road car on the 6th, complainant alleged that defendant was smoking on the platform of the car and remonstrated with him and pointed out the notice prohibiting smoking on that part of the car. In the course of an altercation which ensued the complainant said 'it's no use reasoning with a pig'. Both the complainant and the defendant got off the car at Grove Street and the complainant alleged that the defendant struck him a violent blow on the head which knocked him over. When he regained his feet he saw his assailant running away.

Shepherd was found guilty and fined 7s 6d, plus costs.

MARCH 9TH

1925: The Liverpool Empire theatre opened with a performance of Julian Wylie's *Better Days*.

The Empire was built on the site of an earlier theatre that had been there from 1867 until its closure in February 1924. It was originally the New Prince of Wales, then the Royal Alexandra and latterly the Empire.

The new theatre claimed to have the largest stage in Britain and had 25 per cent more seats than its predecessor. The *Liverpool Daily Courier* reported the following day:

> The new Empire theatre was crowded to the doors at its first opening last night; each of the rose coloured seats was occupied and the business of the stage went on with its accompaniment of sound, light and colour for more than the two hours traffic of which Shakespeare sang. Into the night has gone the old Alexandra. May the new Empire enjoy the sunshine for a long and perfect day.

With further improvements in recent times, the Empire remains one of the country's premier theatres, hosting leading West End musicals. During the years it has also hosted concerts by Bing Crosby, Frank Sinatra and The Beatles.

MARCH 10TH

1884: Seventeen-year-old Michael McLean was hanged for the murder of Spanish sailor Exequiel Nunez.

On 5 January Nunez had been out drinking with his friend Jose Jiminez when they were attacked on Regent Road. Jiminez managed to escape but Nunez was chased and caught at Fulton Street, where he was beaten and stabbed in the neck. Five youths faced trial for his murder, with many of their associates giving evidence trying to lessen the impact each had played in the killing. Three were acquitted but McLean and Patrick Duggan (aged eighteen), were sentenced to death. Duggan was reprieved as he hadn't actually carried out the stabbing but despite his age McLean, who was in possession of the murder weapon when he was arrested, was shown no mercy.

The executioner, Bartholomew Binns, appeared nervous but refused assistance. He miscalculated the drop, and it took ten minutes for McLean to die. The next day's *Liverpool Daily Courier* stated that at the inquest Major Legget, Walton Gaol's governor, said that 'Binns has no idea what he is about' and that he had been drunk on arrival two days earlier. *The Times* reported that Binns took a cab from the gaol to Lime Street station and drank in a number of pubs afterwards, showing off his rope before heading to the platform, where he was nearly refused carriage due to his condition. He was sacked by the Home Office four days later.

MARCH 11TH

1967: Over 100,000 fans flocked to Anfield and Goodison Park as Everton met Liverpool in the 5th round of the FA Cup.

With Liverpool being 1st Division Champions and Everton FA Cup holders, there was unprecedented demand for tickets and in addition to 64,000 inside Goodison, 40,000 watched the game on closed-circuit television at Anfield.

The night before the game, the *Liverpool Echo* reported that fans were paying as much as £5 on the black market for a 5s ground ticket, and that one of the eight giant screens at Anfield had ripped in the wind as it was being put up. The biggest traffic and crowd-control operation ever seen in the city was arranged by police, with overspill car parks operating in Lower Breck Road and Walton Hall Park.

The match didn't live up to expectations, an Alan Ball goal just before half time winning it for Everton. The *Echo* reported on 13 March:

The electric atmosphere, packed Goodison, television relay to Anfield all made it one of the great occasions in Merseyside sporting history but the football content was so inadequate I felt sorry for the thousands who had struggled to get a ticket, struggled through traffic and had to watch a game ruined by a gale and the inability of both teams to sustain any sort of attacking play.

MARCH 12TH

1904: The first trains ran on the newly electrified railway between Liverpool and Southport, the first mainline electric railway in Britain.

This route was chosen as Southport was fast becoming a popular residential area and tourist resort. The electrification of the line, using a third rail, meant journey times for stopping services would be reduced from fifty-four to thirty-seven minutes and an hourly express taking just twenty-five minutes was also planned.

The *Daily Post* reported on 14 March: 'On an experimental run on the electrified portion of the Lancashire and Yorkshire Railway from Liverpool to Southport on Saturday a speed of 60mph was developed.'

The trials paved the way for passenger services to begin on 22 March. Electric trains followed to Ormskirk in 1913 and these two lines are still in existence today as part of Merseyrail's Northern Line, although there is no Southport express service.

MARCH 13TH

1902: The David Lewis Northern Hospital opened on this day.

In the 1880s it became apparent that a new hospital for the north of the city was needed as the one in Great Howard Street was deteriorating. In 1886 building work began between Great Howard Street and Leeds Street, the hospital to be named the David Lewis Northern Hospital due to the financial support received from the David Lewis Trust. Lewis was a merchant and philanthropist who had founded the Lewis's store and had died in 1885.

The hospital was opened by the late Queen Victoria's daughter Princess Louise and her husband the Duke of Argyll. The next day's *Liverpool Mercury* reported of the visit:

> The Princess Louise and the Duke of Argyll yesterday concluded their visit to Liverpool and Knowsley and left for London. The Princess filled a brilliant function by ceremonially opening the David Lewis Northern Hospital. Before leaving the city Her Royal Highness expressed through the Lord Mayor great pleasure at the heartiness of her reception, the Duke adding his own thanks.

The hospital remained open until 1978 when it closed after the Royal Liverpool University Hospital was built.

MARCH 14TH

1948: Thousands flocked to Aintree Racecourse for the first 'Jump Sunday' in eight years.

The racecourse had been requisitioned during the Second World War and was used as a storage depot and a base for American soldiers. The Grand National had been running again since 1946 but this was the first post-war Jump Sunday, when the public were allowed in to inspect the fences.

The following day's *Daily Post* reported that police estimated the crowd was greater than in pre-war years and that at 4 p.m., an hour before the gates closed, Melling Road was 'packed tight with a moving mass of sightseers'. Crowds picnicked and in the brilliant sunshine there were plenty of ice-cream sellers, as well as tipsters writing out Grand National tips on slips of paper for 3*d* a time.

Of the course itself, the *Post* reported that: 'The turf was in fine condition, with the fences trimmed beautifully for the meticulous requirements of the National Hunt Committee. The focal point of interest was naturally Becher's Brook.'

Jump Sunday is no longer an Aintree tradition, having been abandoned after 1960 due to vandalism of the fences.

MARCH 15TH

1926: A sad discovery was made in Anfield when a recluse was found dead in her home.

The following day's *Liverpool Daily Courier* reported that police believed Margaret Ramsey, who lived in Clapham Road, had been dead for about a month. Her body was discovered lying in the kitchen.

The *Courier* reported that she was a virtual stranger to neighbours despite having lived there for three years, with one neighbour telling the paper:

> She was a strange woman and she had nothing to say to anyone. She came here about three years ago but during that time I only saw her on a few occasions. Apparently she was well off because she frequently went away for months at a time. That was why no notice was taken of her door being locked for the past few weeks.

The paper went on to say:

> Police believe she comes from Southampton and have communicated with an address there. When the police entered the house yesterday the gas was still on. It is surmised that Miss Ramsey collapsed as she was lighting the fire. She lived alone and had a charwoman in to do her work but the charwoman had not been there for the last month.

MARCH 16TH

1972: Elder Dempster's liner *Aureol* sailed from the Prince's Landing stage for the last time, meaning Liverpool had no passenger liner services left.

Since the Second World War shipping lines had been cutting back on Liverpool services, leaving the *Aureol*'s service to West Africa as the last one left. However, with sailings only every six weeks it was uneconomical for the Mersey Docks and Harbour Board to continue the upkeep of the landing stage. That evening the *Liverpool Echo* reported:

> Today the graceful liner *Aureol*, the flagship of the Elder Dempster fleet and the last of the great liners to ply from the Prince's Landing Stage, says a farewell to the Mersey and writes 'finis' to a proud era in Liverpool's maritime history. It was in Liverpool that the age of luxury afloat came into being with the introduction of steamships on the North Atlantic. We can truly claim to have seen it all. The port of Liverpool has today said goodbye to some of the glamour that contributed to its greatness.

The *Aureol* sailed between Southampton and West Africa for two more years before the route was ended by Elder Dempster. She went on to become a hotel ship in Saudi Arabia before being broken up in India in 2001.

MARCH 17TH

1980: Protestors staging a sit-in at the Meccano factory in Binns Road, Wavertree, were evicted by bailiffs.

Meccano had been a fixture in the city since 1901, but in November 1979 the company announced the factory would close – with the loss of 900 jobs – as production switched to France and China.

A sit-in was organised, and by the time a court order was secured to allow the bailiffs to gain entry it had reached its 102nd day as a hardened group of workers refused to leave. That day, under the headline BAILIFFS SMASH MECCANO SIT-IN, the *Liverpool Echo* reported that:

> The bailiffs turned up at the occupied toy factory shortly after 5 o'clock this morning and smashed their way through a locked door. Caught unawares, the factory occupying force, just four men, were ushered out and day 102 of the occupation saw the start of a picket at the gates of the Binns Road plant.

The factory was then put up for sale and later demolished to make way for re-development.

MARCH 18TH

1970: A deal was signed for the construction of Liverpool's largest hotel to date as it was announced that a Holiday Inn would be built in Paradise Street. That night's *Liverpool Echo* reported that:

> Work starts next month on a £1.5 million 300 bedroomed luxury hotel with heated indoor pool. It will be the city's largest hotel and each room will have a bathroom, television, radio, air conditioning and two double beds. Top officials of Holiday Inns flew into Liverpool today to sign the building agreement with the Corporation. They were met at the Municipal Annexes in Dale Street by the Leader of the City Council, Alderman Macdonald Steward, and Mr Fred Lloyd from the Corporation's Development Section.

Holiday Inn executives said that about 200 people would be employed when the hotel was finished in 1972 and that 'even the manager they hope would be a local man'.

The Holiday Inn would go on to have many famous guests, including several new Liverpool FC signings. It later became the Moat House and it was demolished to make way for the Liverpool One development.

MARCH 19TH

1866: The *Monarch of the Seas* set sail from Liverpool bound for New York. She was never seen or heard of again, and it is assumed that she perished with 738 persons on board. The *Anglo-American Times* of 14 July reported that:

> If it is true, as appears all but certain, that the *Monarch of the Seas* has perished with all on board, one of the most awful shipwrecks ever occurred has recorded. A lifeboat believed to be hers has been washed up on the coast of Kerry and the bodies of several emigrants, though the state in which they were found rendered identification impossible. All has closed in utter darkness and the *Monarch of the Seas* passes into that category with the *President* and other doomed ships, whose end is known to Him alone, whom even the winds and the sea obey.

On 28 July the same publication reported that a bottle had been found at Devonport with a note inside giving a clue as to where and when she ran into trouble. It stated: '*Monarch of the Seas*, left Liverpool 19th March. May 2nd, no wind, short of provisions and no water. In a gale 3rd April lat 25 deg 20 min N, long 47 min 8 min W – Wm Johnson passenger.'

This would actually place the ship near the Tropics and it is likely the passenger was confused, as 47 latitude and 25 longitude would be in the North Atlantic.

MARCH 20TH

1920: A local football player, Samuel Shepherd, appeared in court after assaulting a referee during a game.

Shepherd was a player for Rowley's United, who were losing a Bootle League Cup tie 5-1 against Boothroyd's at North Park. After being warned for improper conduct in the first half, he was ordered to leave the field for tripping an opposition player as full time neared.

The *Liverpool Daily Courier* reported how the court heard that: 'Shepherd went to the touchline but immediately returned and struck the referee a terrific blow under the jaw. The official dropped senseless and didn't recover consciousness for fifty minutes.'

Shepherd was fined £3 and ordered to pay £2 10s compensation. He was told by the magistrates as sentence was passed: 'If you can't play the game in a sporting spirit and control yourself you had better not play at all.'

MARCH 21ST

1906: A man unexpectedly got a free pair of boots after some strange goings-on in Lord Street.

Under the headline 'AN EXTRAORDINARY SCENE IN LIVERPOOL', the following day's *Liverpool Daily Courier* shared the story:

A scene of the most extraordinary character was witnessed in Lord Street about three o'clock yesterday afternoon, when a young man, evidently belonging to the ranks of the unemployed, stopped in the middle of the street and proceeded to take off his boots and stockings. One of the boots he turned into a missile and directed it at the head of a workman who was repairing a shop blind. The other boot he threw towards Castle Street. The next act on part of this eccentric gentleman was to roll up his trousers, take his coat off and march down Lord Street in the direction of Church Street. Quite a crowd gathered and looked with amazement at the proceedings but there was one onlooker who having an eye to business, appropriated the cast off boots and stockings with the remark 'that fellow may be mad but his boots are better than mine and if he doesn't want 'em I do'. The attention of the police was speedily called to the man and they gave him the attention he evidently required.

MARCH 22ND

1907: Twenty-four people were injured when a train failed to stop at Lime Street station and hit a stationary one.

The accident occurred at 11.15 a.m. and involved a train arriving from Birmingham failing to come to a stop and colliding with six stationary coaches on the line. The guard and twenty-three passengers were injured and had to be treated for shock and cuts and bruises. The following day's *Liverpool Daily Courier* reported:

> A mishap which might easily have been ended by most serious results occurred at 11.15 yesterday morning in Lime Street Station. As it is however some few passengers suffered from shock and the rolling stock although damaged, was not to any great extent. Although none were thought to be seriously injured some few complained of being more or less severely shaken. A gang of workmen were soon headed to the spot and coaches got into a position so they could be removed.

The report into the collision concluded that the fault lay with the driver of the Birmingham train, who had failed to see a flag exhibited from the signal box indicating that a train was already on the platform. As a consequence, he had failed to slow down sufficiently to allow enough time to bring the train to a stop earlier than normally required.

MARCH 23RD

1972: It was a miracle nobody was killed when a bus careered out of control and down an embankment in Bowring Park Road near Broadgreen station, coming to a halt just yards from the railway line.

After taking a left-hand bend the engine started racing, and despite his best efforts the driver was unable to bring it back under control. The bus smashed through a brick wall and careered down the embankment. The accident left eleven people needing treatment in hospital and train services were delayed as the double-decker bus was pulled back up the embankment.

That evening's *Liverpool Echo* included a local resident's eye-witness account: 'I heard a terrific bang. I looked out of the window and saw the bus going through the wall. I ran over and found a child walking round the embankment in a state of shock. She kept saying, "I'm on my way to school". I looked after her until the ambulance arrived.'

In addition to those injured on the bus, another man was injured running to help, spraining his ankle as he fell on the embankment.

MARCH 24TH

1824: Jesse Hartley was appointed Deputy Dock Surveyor in Liverpool, an appointment that was to reap the city huge rewards.

Hartley hailed from Pontefract in West Yorkshire and had mainly worked on bridges before his appointment as deputy to John Foster. However, Foster resigned just three days later, leading to Hartley being promoted on a temporary basis to Dock Surveyor, a position which was confirmed as his the following November. *Billinge's Advertiser* wrote on 20 March: 'The election of Deputy Surveyor and Engineer to the Dock Trustees took place on Wednesday last, when Mr Jesse Hartley, the present Bridgemaster for the Hundred of Salford, was appointed.'

Hartley was one of fifteen applicants, all of whom gave presentations, but he was the overwhelming winner of the vote, receiving the backing of all councillors bar two. During his tenure, which lasted until 1860, the Liverpool docks system quadrupled in size and he developed fireproof warehouses, locks so that ships could be unloaded whether the tide was in or out, and increased the size of the boundary walls to reduce theft.

MARCH 25TH

1807: An Act of Parliament abolished the Slave Trade, something that had brought Liverpool a great deal of prosperity in previous years.

As Royal Assent was given to the Act for the Abolition of the Slave Trade, it meant that slavery would become illegal with effect from the 1 May 1807.

Liverpool merchant and banker William Roscoe had been campaigning for abolition for twenty years, publishing *The Wrongs of Africa* and *A General View of the African Slave Trade* in 1788. As MP for Liverpool (1806-07) he had voted for abolition in the Commons, to the dismay of many in the town who felt it was against its interests. However, he did tell the House of Commons on 20 February that the house was: 'Bound to consider the situation of those who should suffer from the annihilation of a system so long sanctioned by the Legislature.'

Liverpool continued to prosper after abolition, contrary to what many had predicted. The ghosts of the trade can still be seen around the city, though, as many streets are named after slave traders.

MARCH 26TH

1867: A Liverpool policeman was sentenced before the courts for desertion. The following day's *Liverpool Mercury* reported:

Joseph Hill, Police Constable number 93 of the Liverpool force, was brought before Messrs Woodruff and Crosfield at the instance of Superintendent Brennan, charged with desertion from the force. The prisoner joined the force on 15th November 1866 and on the 22nd instant he withdrew himself from the duties of Constable without asking the permission of the Watch Committee and without giving a month's notice to Major Greig. He was apprehended on Monday on board the *Great Eastern* where he was at work and intended to work his passage to New York and thence to Paris. He was fined sixty shillings and costs, in default of payment imprisonment for six weeks. The fine was paid.

MARCH 27TH

1898: The last Sunday service took place in St John's church, which was being demolished to make way for St John's Gardens.

Two services took place, one in the morning and one in the evening, both concentrating on the history of the church. All those attending were given printed copies of the sermons preached along with historical memoranda. The following day's *Daily Post* had this to say:

> The services were the closing services in a church which for 120 years had occupied an important position in the city. The growth of the city had compelled most of those who used to live in or near the parish of St John's to migrate from that business centre to localities better equipped for residence. St John's however for the greater part of its existence attracted a considerable congregation and it was to be closed not because it was a deserted church but because it was important to improve and beautify the centre of this great city. It was satisfactory to know that the demolition of St John's under the Liverpool City Churches Act was likely to be followed by the erection of four or five additional churches where they might be required.

The site of the church was covered by St John's Gardens, a much-needed open space in the city centre where statues of many dignitaries were sited.

MARCH 28TH

1849: Maurice Gleeson killed four members of the same household in Leveson Street, leading to the name of the street being changed.

The victims were music teacher Ann Hinrichson, her two children and maid. Mr Hinrichson was away captaining a ship between Liverpool and Calcutta. The following day's *Liverpool Mercury*, under the headline 'ATROCIOUS AND APPALLING MURDERS IN LEVESON STREET', revealed:

> The annals of crime in this town have been stained by one of the most foul and bloody deeds which it was ever our painful duty to record. A lady far advanced in pregnancy, her two children and waiting maid have been cruelly butchered by a monster in human shape. The two children are dead, of the mother no hopes are entertained and it is only barely possible that the girl might survive her injuries. The appalling spectacle which presented itself to the men who entered was sufficient to overcome with horror the stoutest heart.

The maid, Mary Parr, was able to give a statement to police before she died identifying Gleeson, who had just begun lodging with the family. He was found guilty without the jury needing to leave its box and was hanged at Kirkdale in front of a crowd of around 30,000 people. Due to the notoriety of the killings, Leveson Street was later changed to Grenville Street South.

MARCH 29TH

1893: A pub licensee and customer were each landed with a fine at court after a police officer found the premises in Chisenhale Street open during prohibited hours. The following day's *Daily Post* reported that:

> An inspector said he found the door of the defendant's house open at 12.15 on the day in question. He entered the premises and there found a man at the bar with a pint of beer before him. Witness noticed that the clock in the room indicated the time of 12.30 and upon pointing this out to the defendant, who was unaware that this clock was wrong, he immediately took back the glass of beer, none of which was drunk and returned the money.

The solicitor for James Maxwell, the licensee, caused much laughter in the room when he claimed that Maxwell must have been closing the pub early at night too. But this cut no ice with the magistrate, who told him that he needed to take steps to determine the time before imposing a fine of 10s. The customer William Ashton, who was charged with 'being on licensed premises during prohibited hours', claimed he had seen the door open and ordered a pint, but not paid for or drunk it. He was fined 5s.

MARCH 30TH

1900: The Prince of Wales was at Aintree to see his horse triumph in the Grand National.

The following day's *Liverpool Mercury* revealed that the Prince had stayed at Knowsley Hall, and that 'the greatest enthusiasm prevailed along the route to the course' as he made his way in an open brougham escorted by mounted police. The Prince's presence attracted a record crowd to the course, where the Liverpool Constabulary Band performed in between races. 'As the hour approached for the race,' the *Mercury* added, 'the scene amongst the paddock, enclosures, county and members stands was of a brilliant description. Many well-known ladies of fashion were present and their presence lent an additional interest to proceedings.'

The Prince sat in the Lord Derby stand to see his horse, Ambush II, win the race, amidst tremendous enthusiasm and waving of hats and handkerchiefs. After watching other races, the Prince returned to Knowsley for the night. The skeleton of Ambush II is now on display at the Museum of Liverpool.

MARCH 31ST

1788: A large crowd attended the first execution in Liverpool since 1715.

The previous Christmas Eve, Silvester Dowling and Patrick Byrne, armed with pistols and knives, broke into a house in Rose Hill, tied up their victims and ransacked the house before fleeing with silverware and cash. They were later arrested in Bristol whilst awaiting a boat to Dublin. After being found guilty at Lancaster and sentenced to death, the Liverpool authorities – determined to set an example – erected a gallows in Water Street. On 7 April Williamson's *Advertiser* reported:

> A little after ten o'clock the prisoners, attended by the Under-Sheriff, a clergyman and other officers were brought by a passage erected for the purpose from the gaol to the platform, which were hung with black for the occasion, and after a few minutes spent in devotion they were launched into Eternity to make their appearance before the Throne of that JUST yet MERCIFUL GOD who we sincerely hope will accept their pertinence and sufferings as atonement for their guilt.

Up to 20,000 people were present, the *Advertiser* commenting: 'It is our moral ardent that this public example may affect the end for which it is designed, by deferring the guilty from a perseverance in the commission of such crimes.'

APRIL 1ST

1974: Merseyside County Council and Merseyside Police came into being. That evening's *Liverpool Echo* reported: 'It was all change today for local government on Merseyside. Replacing more than twenty-five councils a new county council begins to operate with five district councils. People living in the new areas, from Southport to Wirral, Bootle over to St Helens are now in a new postal district called Merseyside'.

As part of the shake-up, police forces were to run along council boundaries, meaning that the Liverpool and Bootle Police, itself only in existence since 1967, joined forces with parts of Lancashire and Cheshire Police. The *Echo* welcomed the changes, commenting: 'The pattern of local government which has stood substantially unaltered for eight-four years has shot overnight into the twentieth century. The massive new metropolitan units now provide local governments with greater freedom of action than it has ever engaged in the past.'

Although Merseyside still exists as a county, it has no overall governing body, having ceased to exist in 1986 with powers being devolved to the individual councils. Merseyside Police continues to enforce the law in the region, with more than 4,000 officers.

APRIL 2ND

1977: Red Rum won the Grand National for the third time. 'Rummie', trained by Ginger McCain on the sands at Southport, had won the race in 1973 and 1974 then finished second in the next two years. At the age of twelve, many feared he was too old to win the gruelling race for a third time, but speculative betting shortened the odds to a relatively slight 9-1 (compared to 15-2 for the favourite, Andy Pandy).

After romping to victory by 25 lengths, that evening's *Football Echo* declared him the greatest Grand National horse of all time and described how he had 'stormed to the line leaving the rest trailing in his wake'. The win won a Formby punter a whopping £39,000 (against a stake of £200 double on the Cheltenham Gold Cup and Grand National).

Red Rum was due to compete in the next year's race, but suffered a hairline fracture the day before and pulled out. His three victories though went a long way to restoring the race's popularity after many years of decline. He was a regular visitor to the course for many more years and after he died, in 1995, he was buried near the winning post.

April 3rd

1928: The Mayors of Liverpool and Birkenhead shook hands under the Mersey after the breakthrough had occurred in the construction of the Queensway tunnel.

Construction had begun in December 1925 after an Act of Parliament and 1,700 workers were involved in the project. It was decided to build a tunnel rather than a bridge across the Mersey, due to it being cheaper and less vulnerable to attack in wartime. The breakthrough had actually occurred the previous week, however, and this was merely a staged ceremony and photo opportunity. The front page of the following day's *Liverpool Daily Courier* was covered with photographs and its report of the occasion read:

> Sir Archibald Salvidge, Chairman of the Mersey Tunnel Joint Committee, bored through the four inch wall of red sandstone rock 150 feet below the Mersey and united Liverpool and Birkenhead. A squad of expert workmen sweated at their task of smashing a passage through the wall. The Lord Mayor of Liverpool, Margaret Beavan, attired in the regulation oilskin outfit with the addition of a chain of office, stood on the raised platform ready to greet the Birkenhead Mayoral party when the gap was wide enough to pass through. A great cheer was raised on both sides when the hole through was accomplished and immediately the two Mayors exchanged greetings, joining hands in *Auld Lang Syne*.

APRIL 4TH

1950: Customs officers seized a large number of stockings on board a liner at Liverpool docks.

The stockings were hidden in various places on board the Cunard liner *Franconia*. The following evening's *Liverpool Echo* had this to add:

Customs officers were still busily engaged today counting the haul. Enquiries following the seizure are said to be confined to the Merseyside area. The stockings are said to be nylons. The discovery was made last evening on board the *Franconia*, newly arrived from New York via Halifax. Rummage crews of customs men, suspecting a large scale attempt, searched the vessel continuously from time of her arrival at Prince's landing stage on Monday morning until the discovery was made in the docks last night. The stockings were in cellophane packages and concealed on several parts of the ship.

APRIL 5TH

1929: The desperate daily struggle to find work hit home when 500 men looking to be taken on as dockers or fruit porters fought each other at Wapping Dock.

That evening's *Evening Express* reported: '500 men literally fought each other for a day's work early today and police reinforcements were relinquished to dispose them. Discoloured eyes, bruises and abrasions, kicked legs and shins were plentiful.' The men were hoping to be taken on to unload 35,000 cases of Jaffa oranges, and the drama began at about 7.30 a.m. when the timekeeper arrived. He was immediately surrounded by men and then carried into the crowd, being rescued by police.

A total of 200 men were taken on and the other 300 left, one telling the paper:

> It was a good scrap whilst it lasted. I would not be bothered about a couple of black eyes if only I could have got a day's work. I have a wife and eight little children at home. I know that all 500 men couldn't be taken on the job but when the fight started I thought I might as well take a chance.

APRIL 6TH

1958: Merseysiders shivered on Easter Sunday as Britain was gripped by cold weather. Under the headline 'FIRESIDE EASTER', the following day's *Daily Post* revealed:

> Although in some places Saturday's Arctic weather gave way yesterday to slightly more tolerable conditions it was the coldest Easter Sunday in London this century. Even last Christmas Day was warmer. On Merseyside the thermometer reached 47. Traffic on the roads was far below that on a normal Easter Sunday and the railways were never at any time busy.

The paper went on to say that on the Mersey ferries, passengers numbers were only half what they were in 1957 and that many people cancelled planned coach excursions due to the weather. A British Railways spokesman at Lime Street station said it was the quietest Easter Sunday for years with passenger numbers 'only a fleabite to what we usually carry at Easter'.

At Southport only six people were brave enough to hire deckchairs whilst in Wirral: 'The promenades at Hoylake and West Kirby did not present the usual happy picture of bumper to bumper parking.'

APRIL 7TH

1885: A sale of work was held at St Margaret's church in Rocky Lane, which was aiming to clear a £400 debt.

The following day's *Liverpool Mercury* reported that the Lord Mayor, Alderman David Radcliffe, opened the event, which featured stalls selling household items and ornaments made and donated by the parishioners themselves. He commended their skills, saying: 'Though they may be poor monetarily they were rich in good work and was a proof of their industry and willingness of good heart.' The paper reported that the Revd J. Sheepshanks told those present of the wider role the church played in the local community: 'The hall is used on Sundays for children's mission and adults' mission services and for bible classes. The St Margaret's Young Men's Club is also held there.'

Those present were entertained by a military band and the stalls were run by local dignitaries and their wives.

APRIL 8TH

1896: The funeral of merchant and shipping magnate George Holt took place on this day. Holt was the son of a cotton broker and co-founded the Lamport and Holt Line in 1845, which traded with India, South Africa and South America. In 1884 Holt moved to Sudley House in Mossley Hill, acquiring a large number of paintings and also giving generously to many local educational establishments. The following day's *Liverpool Mercury* described his funeral:

> The cortege left the Holt residence shortly after two o' clock and all along the route the long procession of carriages were watched with the most respectful interest. The service in the chapel was brief and of the simplest character being conducted with conformity for the order of the Unitarian faith. The coffin, almost hidden by the beautiful amount of wreaths, was carried from the chapel to the grave by six of the firm's employees.

After Holt's death his daughter Emma continued his legacy of philanthropy, and when she died in 1944, leaving no descendants, Sudley Hall and its paintings were left to the City of Liverpool.

April 9th

1869: Author Charles Dickens gave his last reading in Liverpool, having been a regular visitor since he sailed from here to the America in 1842.

By 1869 Dickens's health was failing and he struggled to eat solid food, and as such the tour was billed as a farewell one:

> Mr Charles Dickens made his final bow to the Liverpool audience in the character of a public reader. We question whether he ever received a more numerous and appreciative audience than that which filled nearly every seat in the spacious Theatre Royal. He read the terrible story of *Sikes and Nancy* with, as it seemed to us, more fire and force than he had shown before during the week. The final reading was *A Christmas Carol,* so well suited for such an occasion for it gave Mr Dickens an opportunity of taking leave of the audience in the simple affectionate words of Tiny Tim: 'God bless us everyone'. So earnest was the applause at the close of the reading that Mr Dickens was compelled to return to the stage and bow his acknowledgements.
>
> (*Liverpool Mercury*)

Two weeks after leaving Liverpool he suffered a stroke in Preston and had to cancel the rest of the tour. He died at home in June 1870, never regaining consciousness after a second stroke.

APRIL 10TH

1919: The mass movement of troops returning home after the First World War continued as 3,000 Canadian soldiers left Liverpool. Although the war had finished the previous November, the sheer number of troops involved meant repatriation of those from other continents took time. The following day's *Liverpool Daily Courier* described the departure:

> A further big contingent of Canadian soldiers sailed home from Liverpool yesterday on board the Cunard liner *Carmania*. The troops, who numbered nearly 3,000, were the famous Canadian Guards of the First Division, many of whom were fighting for the Empire in 1914. Major General A. C. MacDonnell, in command of the Division, stood at the gangway as the men went on board the ship and wished them a cordial 'bon voyage'.
>
> (*Evening Express*)

Each soldier was presented with a booklet detailing the Division's battles during the war, with a personal message from General MacDonnell which said:

> The 1st Canadian Division has proved on many a bloody triumphant field that it is the last word in efficiency and uniformly successful. I cannot view the break-up of my beautiful 1st Canadian Division with equanimity. It breaks me up to. That is the truth. Canada is proud of you and Canada is grateful.

APRIL 11TH

1947: The Students' Congress met in Liverpool and discussed the plight of sick students. That evening's *Evening Express* reported that a London student had told the Congress: 'Students were ill and unable to get food except for a few biscuits. The sick student, perhaps suffering from flu, was compelled to stagger down to a café for food or stay in bed for days without.'

Attendees called for landladies to provide food for students who were sick; if they refused, sick wards should be made available in universities where they could be fed, and a lodgings' officer hired to inspect accommodation. A Liverpool student disputed a claim that students were one of the more healthy groups in society, suggesting: 'If this was so it was a reflection on the general health of the community. Students are not a healthy body unless you call it healthy merely to stagger from lecture to lecture or go in search of food.'

To address the general health problem as a whole, the Congress called for medical officers to be appointed in all universities and for students to be examined on enrolment.

APRIL 12TH

1827: George Canning, MP for Liverpool, became prime minister. Canning succeeded the Earl of Liverpool, who had been forced to step down on health grounds. It was the culmination of a long-running power struggle. His rise to the prime-ministerial role led to the resignation of Chancellor Lord Eldon and Billinge's *Advertiser* was more than happy with the situation, commenting on 17 April:

Our readers will see with great satisfaction that the long and arduous struggle for ascendency in the Cabinet has at length terminated in the complete triumph of Mr Canning and they will perhaps see with equal satisfaction that Lord Eldon and his party have resigned. The triumph of Mr Canning has long been anticipated and of course excited more satisfaction than surprise. Among those ministers who have resigned there is no one except Mr Peel who will at all be regretted. The country is with Mr Canning and will we hope support him against all his enemies.

Canning's period in office turned out to be an extremely short one, as he died on 8 August 1827. Canning Street in Liverpool is named after him.

APRIL 13TH

1954: Liverpool Corporation announced measures to clamp down on fare dodgers on public transport, which they claimed was costing them 3 per cent of their budget, or £140,000 a year.

The following day's *Daily Post* reported that the Passenger Transport Committee (PTC) proposed to increase the number of inspectors proportionally to take into account the extra number of trams and buses on the roads since they were first introduced in 1947. It also included that Mr W.M. Hall, the General Manager of the PTC, had recommended that: 'Ticket checking staff should be given prospects of promotion at least open to those inspectors on other work. This would encourage a better type of man to undertake ticket checking.'

Hall stated that although the proposed changes would cost £10,000 a year there was a potential to recoup a net £37,000 in losses if fare dodging could be cut to 2 per cent of income (from 3 per cent).

APRIL 14TH

1930: An after-hour's drinking den was closed down by magistrates and two men imprisoned for assaulting police officers who had raided it.

According to an *Evening Express* report, police officers had attended the Edge Hill Social Club on Shenstone Street and been attacked by customers, forcing them to draw their batons. The husband and wife who ran the club were both charged in relation to the incident, with the husband, John Walsh, being accused of both assault and aiding and abetting his wife to sell beer without a licence. Mr Walsh was fined £4, his wife £3 10s; their twenty-one-year-old son received a fine of 40s. Two customers each received three months' gaol with hard labour for assaulting the police, while five others were given fines of 10s and 20s for consuming beer after hours. The *Echo* described how the magistrate also 'struck the club off the register on the grounds of illegal sales of liquor. The premises were also disqualified from club purposes for twelve months.'

APRIL 15TH

1989: One of the darkest moments in Liverpool's history occurred when ninety-six Liverpool FC fans were killed at the FA Cup semi-final at Hillsborough, Sheffield.

Those who died were crushed to death when a gate to the stadium was opened, allowing more supporters into an already overcrowded area. Ninety-four fans died on the day; another person perished on 19 April and a ninety-sixth, Mr Tony Bland, remained in a coma for four years before his life support was switched off in 1993. On 16 April a special edition of the *Liverpool Echo* was published, saying that:

> Thousands rushed onto the terrace with the force of a guided missile. Hillsborough was suddenly plunged into sheer horror. The full horror of what had happened quickly became apparent. Spectators tore up advertising hoardings to use as impromptu stretchers. The tall fencing installed to keep spectators off the pitch only made matters worse because it prevented people escaping.

The subsequent Taylor Report blamed a failure of police control for the disaster, but the inquest returned a verdict of accidental death. Today relatives of the dead and survivors of the disaster are still campaigning for the full facts to be made available and a fresh inquest.

APRIL 16TH

1930: Magistrates granted a licence for the Crown Hotel in Norris Green, the first on the new estate to be granted.

The issue of licenced premises in the area was a contentious one. The solicitors for the applicants pointed out that despite the number of new corporation houses built in the area there were no licensed premises within half a mile (compared to London Road, which had over 700 within the same distance). It was pointed out that The Crown was not to be just a pub, but also:

> … a refreshment house for users of two great roads, where meals and tea and coffee will also be sold at reasonable prices. For lorry drivers there will be a drying room for dying clothes and cubicles where they could sleep in an annexe. [He] advised that it wasn't to be situated on the estate itself but next to it, [that] 75 per cent of the residents of the housing estate were in favour of the application and that they should expect similar facilities and amenities as other parts of the city enjoyed.

Magistrates granted the licence and the Crown Hotel was built at a cost of £14,000. It was demolished in 2007.

APRIL 17TH

1951: A man who had shot his wife and mother-in-law the previous day turned the gun on himself when the police caught up with him.

Walter Ray Beech had carried out the shootings in Underley Street, Wavertree. Despite his notoriety, the day afterwards he met a girl in Toxteth and took her to lunch and the cinema before having a drink with her in the Prince's Park pub in Upper Stanhope Street. Two detectives carrying out routine checks of pubs came across a man fitting Beech's description at 6 p.m. on 17 April:

> They challenged him but were not satisfied with his reply, as he gave a false name and address. The detectives took him to another room where it is stated he drew a revolver and shouted 'stand back or you'll get it'. The detectives made to close with him but before they could get to grips he turned the revolver and shot himself. The bullet passed clean through his head and into the next room. The sound of the shot was the signal for hundreds of neighbours and their children to collect at the street corner and peer through upper windows as police cars and ambulances arrived.
>
> (*Daily Post*)

Beech was pronounced dead at the scene and his body taken to a mortuary.

APRIL 18TH

1966: Liverpool was brought an hour closer to London with the introduction of electric trains on the rail service to the capital. The first electric train left Lime Street station at 7.55 a.m. and arrived at London Euston two hours and twenty-seven minutes later, averaging 85mph during the journey. That evening's *Liverpool Echo* describes the scene as the train departed:

> Bandsmen of Edge Hill Railway Band in their plum coloured uniforms blew fanfares on the concourse and again on platform seven which was bedecked with flowers. The story of today's achievement was told in a plaque of coloured blooms worked by the Liverpool Parks Department. The first railway locomotive, the old *Lion*, was depicted as well as the modern electric locomotive in blue hyacinths with the date 1844-1966.

At a commemorative luncheon in London, Barbara Castle, Minister for Transport, told those present: 'Electrification of British Railways was a showpiece indicative of the modernisation of Britain. The new service would stand comparison with rails anywhere.' The time of the service remained the same for forty years and has now been cut to two hours and seven minutes for the fastest journeys.

APRIL 19TH

1883: The Liverpool Society for the Prevention of Cruelty to Children was formed. The local banker Thomas Agnew was behind its formation. He took inspiration from the New York Society for the Prevention of Cruelty to Children after he visited there in 1881. The formation of the society was unanimously approved by a meeting of bankers, councillors, merchants, ministers at the Town Hall. Agnew told those present:

> Mendicants stopped at home and sent their children out into the streets in all weathers and at all times. Such parents ceased to look at their offspring as creatures entrusted to them by God and looked upon them simply as machines for bringing in a quantity of money. Such a society was bound to interfere and do something to protect these helpless little ones.
>
> (*Liverpool Daily Courier*)

In July the following year a London society was established, following guidance from Agnew, and by 1889 there were thirty-two branches throughout England, Scotland and Wales. That year the society became the National Society for the Prevention of Cruelty to Children – NSPCC for short – with Queen Victoria as its patron, and it continues its good work today.

APRIL 20TH

1912: A memorial service took place at St Peter's church in Church Street to remember those who had lost their lives when the *Titanic* sank five days earlier.

More than 1,500 lives were lost on the ship, owned by Liverpool shipping company the White Star Line, when it struck an iceberg in the North Atlantic en route from Southampton to New York. Those that perished included around 100 people with Liverpool connections. The service was attended by the Lord Mayor of Liverpool, the Mayors of Bootle and Birkenhead and the Bishop of Liverpool. Also present were Mrs Ismay, wife of White Star Line's Chairman J. Bruce Ismay, General Manager Harold Sanderson and his assistant Henry Concanon and up to 400 staff.

A solemn memorial service, which brought home very closely to all taking part in it the awful tragedy of the foundering of the *Titanic,* was held at noon on Saturday in St Peter's church. The sacred edifice was filled with a congregation drawn from all classes of the community, and during the service many of the ladies, who formed the greater proportion, were moved to tears by the pathos of the occasion and the thoughts of all were with the sufferers of the unprecedented calamity of the sea.

(Daily Post and Mercury)

APRIL 21ST

1862: The Liverpool Sailors' Home re-opened after it had been destroyed by fire two years earlier. The home was opened in Canning Place in 1850 to offer seafarers a better standard of accommodation available in many of the city's other lodging houses. It was designed to look like a ship's interior, with rooms running off galleries spread over five floors.

The whole interior had been damaged by the fire, which had been started deliberately. A concert by the Sailors' Home Glee Party marked the re-opening, the next day's *Liverpool Mercury* reporting:

> The re-opening of the building was celebrated by a grand concert, the committee of the institution having sought to provide for the rational entertainment of the sailors during the leisure hours to which they would otherwise be exposed to much temptation. There was a crowded audience including, besides the seamen and their friends, a great number of ladies and gentlemen resident in the town. The songs were as effectively rendered that many of them were loudly encored and all the artistes were greeted in the most cordial manner.

The home eventually closed in 1969 and has now been demolished. In August 2011 the gates, which had been in a museum in Sandwell, were returned to the city and erected near to where it had once stood in Paradise Street.

APRIL 22ND

1899: The Liverpool School of Tropical Medicine (LSTM) was inaugurated. The LSTM was fist founded by ship-owner Sir Alfred Lewis Jones the previous November, when he pledged £350 per year for three years. Initially known as the Liverpool School of Tropical Diseases, it was to be the first of its kind in the world and initially based in buildings leased from the University College of Liverpool. The *Liverpool Daily Courier* reported the opening:

> The inauguration of the Liverpool School for the Study of Tropical Diseases took place on Saturday. Lord Lister when opening at the Royal Southern Hospital, the Samuel Henry Thompson Ward, which has been set apart for the treatment of these cases, pointed out that Liverpool in this matter was doing a work of the greatest benefit to the welfare of mankind. He spoke at the importance of such cases being dealt with at a hospital which was attached to a school for their study.

In 1902 the LSTM found that the spread of malaria was linked to mosquitoes, leading to lecturer Ronald Ross receiving the Nobel Prize for Medicine, and they moved into purpose-built premises in Pembroke Place in 1920. In recent years it has moved to a new state-of-the-art facility, the Centre for Tropical and Infectious Diseases, a stone's throw from its previous site.

APRIL 23RD

1927: Greyhound racing arrived in Liverpool with the opening of the city's first track, Breck Park, in Townsend Lane in Clubmoor. The sport had only been introduced to Britain the previous summer, the first track opening at Belle Vue in Manchester in July 1926. But its popularity was spreading around the country, with 8,000 people attending Liverpool's first meeting.

On 25 April the *Daily Post and Mercury* felt the need to explain the new sport in minute detail, stating:

> You get a hare's skin, stuff it and attach it to an electric contrivance that sends it scurrying round the course as if it were the real thing running for dear life. The dogs chase that thing round until the deceitful unfeeling animal has made an electric dive into an animal hole.

Most of the bets placed were down to lucky numbers, although some rumours did spread around the crowd about form. The paper reported that 'there were six races, [and] in one or two there was a beautifully close finish. In one three dogs passed the post in a heap. In others the result was pretty clear before the race was three quarters through.'

Breck Park stadium was closed in 1948 after it had suffered war damage. Its site is now occupied by Waterloo Dock FC.

APRIL 24TH

1905: The Olympia theatre in West Derby Road opened. It was built as a circus and variety venue and designed to accommodate 3,750 people. In the basement were lifting mechanisms to bring the elephants and lions onto the stage.

The following day's *Liverpool Daily Courier* was enthusiastic about the opening night, which included a performance of the musical *Tally Ho* as well as acts by singers, comedians, dancers and jugglers:

> The success which was so richly deserved attended the opening performances at Olympia, West Derby Road last evening. Probably never in fact has such a whole-hearted enthusiasm been previously displayed in Liverpool at the initial entertainment at any place of amusement. The whole of the vast audience, numbering close on 4,000, for every seat was occupied, raised cheer upon cheer.

The Olympia never lived up to expectations and closed in 1925, re-opening as a cinema until the outbreak of the Second World War in 1939. It has since been used as a bingo hall and nightclub before re-opening in the late 1990s as a theatre and boxing venue with a capacity of up to 1,960.

APRIL 25TH

1796: Local doctor Samuel Solomon placed an advert in Billinge's *Liverpool Advertiser & Marine Intelligence* for his celebrated cordial 'Balm of Gilead'.

Solomon practiced in Marybone and claimed the medicine, priced half a guinea per bottle, could cure plenty of ailments: 'For the relief of nervous disorders, female complaints, weaknesses, loss of appetite, impurity of blood, headaches, relaxation, bilious cases, debility, indigestion, ill-cured lues, seminal weaknesses, coughs and colds, consumptions, lowness of spirits, scorbutic diseases, pains in the limbs, gleets, etc etc.'

The medicine promised to strengthen the stomach, back, weakened organs and whole constitution and that those who had 'brought upon themselves a numerous train of evils will by the use of this find themselves restored to health and strength'. The cordial was made of pure essence of virgin gold and foam of the choicest balsams, and said to be prepared 'only by Dr Solomon MD of the University and College of Physics, Aberdeen and author of *The Guide to Health*'.

Solomon later lived in Kensington in a house named Gilead House which, although no longer there, is remembered today by Balm Street, Gilead Street and Solomon Street.

APRIL 26TH

1842: The power of the Mersey was brought home when three rowers drowned after their boat capsized. The *Liverpool Mercury* of 29 April shared the tragic tale:

> We have this week to record one of the most melancholy and fatal accidents which has occurred in this neighbourhood for some time past, and by which three young men connected with the most respectable circles in the town have met a watery grave. On the morning of Tuesday last five young gentlemen after breakfast at the residence of John Moss Esquire at Otterspool put off in a light rowing gig for the purpose of enjoying the healthful exercise and recreation of rowing. The day was beautifully bright and clear yet there was a good breeze stirring and they found the river somewhat rough. They were laughing and joking at the waves which tossed their boat to and fro. Suddenly they got between two waves, one of which struck the boat and, by some means by which the survivors are unable to surmise, split her open. The weight caused her to turn over. Mr Taunton and Mr Crewe succeeded in seizing hold of the stem and stern, where they managed to cling, but the other unfortunate gentlemen were overwhelmed by the waves and disappeared.

Those that died were Mr A. Littledale, Mr C. Royds and Mr J. Ramsay.

APRIL 27TH

1829: The Liverpool & Manchester Railway Co. announced a £500 prize for whoever designed the locomotive that would be used on the service. With the tracks now nearly ready, trials were set for Rainhill in October to decide how the carriages would be hauled. The competition carried eight stipulations and conditions:

I. That the engine must 'effectively consume its own smoke'.
II. The engine must be capable of drawing after it a train of carriages of the gross weight of twenty tons.
III. There must be two safety valves.
IV. The engine and boiler must be supported on springs.
V. The weight of the machine must not exceed six tons.
VI. There must be a mercurial gauge fitted to the machine.
VII. The engine to be delivered complete for trial not later than the 1 October.
VIII. The price not to exceed £550.

The following October, George Stephenson's *Rocket* wrote itself into history.

APRIL 28TH

1966: Liverpool FC fans hoping to support their team in the following week's European Cup Winners' Cup Final in Glasgow were frustrated when they were told not enough planes were available to meet demand. In the days before the M6 and M74 were completed, the journey to Scotland was an arduous one and many hoped to make the trip to the club's first European final by plane. However, that evening's *Liverpool Echo* bore the bad news, with Harry Langley, director of P&M Travel, telling the paper: 'We just cannot obtain enough planes, we have tried every airline in the British Isles, but there isn't a spare aircraft to be had anywhere.'

The paper reported that Towns Travel had received enough enquiries to fill a dozen more planes, whilst those that had been lucky enough to find a space were paying £9 instead of £6 due to the cost of bringing in aircraft from southern England. Although 30,000 Liverpool fans did make it to Glasgow by a variety of travel methods, they were left disappointed as Borussia Dortmund won the game 2-1.

APRIL 29TH

1908: A Liverpool licensee accused of allowing a drunken man onto his premises saw the case against him dismissed. The following day's *Liverpool Daily Courier* reported the court's proceedings:

William Spurgin, licensee of 61 Soho Street, was summoned for permitting a drunken person to be on his premises on the evening of the 20th. The police evidence was that they had entered the premises and that a man who appeared worse for liquor was sitting on a form in the bar. The police went out and on re-entering by another door they saw the same man falling on the floor as if he had been knocked down. The police drew the licensee's attention to the drunken man and he replied, 'I've told him to get out and he won't go. I've been attending to other customers.' Mr Berry (defending) said that the defendant had ordered a man and a drunken soldier to get out but they refused. The defendant had been a licensee for 24 years and had never been summoned or fined before. The case was dismissed.

APRIL 30TH

1924: A Belfast to Liverpool air-mail service was inaugurated. The service was the first of its kind within the UK and aimed to increase delivery speeds between Northern Ireland and England/Wales. Prices for the sending of letters by airmail and packets were half a penny for every 2oz, on top of the normal penny post fee.

The following week's *Flight Magazine* reported that the plane, which had departed Belfast two hours late because of wet weather there, landed 'to the accompaniment of hearty cheers from the crowd that had gathered at the Aintree aerodrome'. The pilot and his two passengers, the Lord Mayor and High Sheriff of Belfast, then attended a special luncheon at the Town Hall. Belfast's Lord Mayor, Sir William Turner, said: 'I tender greetings to you and the citizens of Liverpool on the inauguration of the air mail service between Belfast and Liverpool. On such an auspicious occasion may I convey to you the good wishes of the people of Belfast and express a great hope that the ties of friendship will be strengthened by this service.'

Sadly the service didn't get the business hoped for and was out of operation by the end of the year.

MAY 1ST

1840: Joseph Williamson, known as the Mole of Edge Hill, died – meaning that several local workmen were now without employment.

Williamson came to Liverpool from Yorkshire aged just eleven in 1780 and became a successful tobacco merchant, moving to (then mainly rural) Edge Hill in 1805, where he developed plenty of properties that he rented out to increase his fortune further. Williamson employed many local men, including ex-soldiers returning from the Napoleonic Wars in 1816, to build a network of tunnels under Edge Hill, simply to provide them with work. This continued until his death in 1840, when all his workers were laid off.

The description of Williamson in *Recollections of Old Liverpool* by James Stonehouse is that he was 'rough and uncouth', which may explain why in the local press his death was not given more than just a couple of lines. The *Liverpool Daily Courier* on 6 May mentioned him in the deaths' section: 'On Friday last, at Edge-hill, Joseph Williamson Esq, age 71', with the *Liverpool Mercury* printing something on similar lines.

MAY 2ND

1984: The Liverpool International Garden Festival opened. Billed as a 'pageant of horticultural excellence and spectacular entertainment', it was developed on previously derelict land. One of the first projects undertaken by the Merseyside Development Corporation, the festival had a miniature railway, pavilions, festival hall and sixty individual gardens. The gardens were opened by Queen Elizabeth II and the Duke of Edinburgh before they went for a ride on the miniature train. The Queen said that the blooming gardens were appropriate for Liverpool's renewal, as plants wither and die in winter but grow again in spring.

The *Liverpool Echo* added more that evening: 'It was "all aboard" in style for the Queen and Prince Philip when they boarded the festival train this morning. The quarter-size steam engine *Samson*, gleaming in its brightly polished red and black colours, pulled the royal carriage around its two and half miles of track.'

The festival went on to attract over 3 million visits before it closed in October. Half the land has since been re-developed into housing, whilst the other half has been used for various leisure schemes.

MAY 3RD

1989: The Eldonian Village in Vauxhall was opened by Prince Charles, the culmination of a battle by local residents to remain in their area. At the start of the decade tenements in Eldon Street and Burlington Street were earmarked for demolition, meaning the residents faced being dispersed throughout the city and beyond. Refusing to accept this, they formed their own housing co-operative, seeking to build on the site of the former Tate & Lyle factory that closed its doors in 1981. They gained the support of local key housing officials and churchmen to be able to influence the government.

When Prince Charles came to open the scheme, Eldonian Chairman Tony McGann told him that each dwelling represented a model that could be used for any inner city in the country. The following day's *Daily Post* reported that Prince Charles praised McGann's 'blunt speaking' as from time to time it was needed. He told those gathered: 'People should see for themselves what has been achieved and take it back to their own areas. You have set a great example for others to follow.'

Now a community-based housing association, the Eldonian scheme has gone on to win several accolades, including the United Nations sponsored World Habitat Award in 2004.

MAY 4TH

1925: The first dedicated juvenile court in the country opened in Liverpool, situated in a purpose-built building in Crosshall Street. It was opened by local politician Sir Archibald Salvidge, who presented Lord Mayor Alderman Thomas Dowd with a golden key in commemoration. The following day's *Liverpool Daily Courier* reported Stipendiary Magistrate Stuart Deacon as saying: 'This is the happiest day I have spent since I became Stipendiary Magistrate. Liverpool was once described as the black spot on Merseyside but I think that with these improvements it will be the brightest and happiest spot on Merseyside.'

The dedicated court was welcomed by the Home Secretary, who wrote a letter of support, whilst Sir Thomas Molony, chairman of a Home Office committee looking at the treatment of juvenile offenders said: 'A new spirit exists to deal with the young, with a juvenile court much can be done to eradicate the cause of these crimes.' Dedicated juvenile courts were soon rolled out across the country and Liverpool Youth Court, as it became known, remained in Crosshall Street until the 1970s, when it moved to Hatton Garden; it is now based in Derby Square.

MAY 5TH

1928: Dixie Dean scored a hat-trick for Everton FC in a 3-3 draw against Arsenal, and achieved the remarkable feat of scoring sixty league goals in a season.

Everton had already been crowned champions, after a late surge saw them overhaul favourites Huddersfield at the top of the table to clinch the title in their penultimate game. If Everton's title was an unlikely one, Dean's achievement was even more spectacular considering with three games left he was only on fifty-one goals. However, he hit two in a 3-2 win at home to Aston Villa and four in a 5-3 win at Burnley to set up the grandstand finish at Goodison Park. Dean's first goal was a header and his second a penalty after he was brought down when through on goal. With just nine minutes to go, he headed himself into history. That evening's *Football Echo* report of the game stated:

> Troup took the corner and out of a ruck of fourteen players Dean, with unerring accuracy, nodded the ball to the right side of the goal. There has never been a more joyful shout at Everton. It was prolonged for minutes and went on to the end of the game. The crowd never stopped cheering for eight solid minutes and Dean was hugged by all his comrades.

Arsenal equalised before the end but it couldn't detract from Dean's feat, something that will surely never be equalled.

MAY 6TH

1941: St Luke's church was bombed as Liverpool suffered a fifth successive night of terror from German bombers. The church, at the bottom of Hardman Street, was hit by an incendiary device shortly after midnight, causing the roof to fall in and a fire to start, destroying most of the interior as well as every one of the stained glass windows. The clock stopped at 3.36 a.m., the time the fire reached the upper storeys of the tower.

So as not to affect morale or give the Germans any indication of the damage being caused, newspapers at the time were deliberately vague when it came to reporting the consequences of the raids. As such the *Liverpool Echo* was no more specific than saying:

> Some fires were started but these were speedily tackled. A spectacular one was at a church where the ever changing patterns of the flames as seen in the many windows appearing like living stained glass. The church was one of the oldest in Liverpool. The lectern, a memorial desk and a number of altar cloths were saved. The bells crashed to the floor and all the stained glass windows were wrecked.

Today the church remains as an empty shell, standing as a memorial to the victims of the May Blitz.

MAY 7TH

1951: At Anfield Cemetery a civic memorial was unveiled dedicated to the victims of the Liverpool Blitz, six years after the end of the Second World War. The memorial was unveiled over a communal grave where many unknown victims of the raids had been buried. The following day's *Daily Post* reported that the Bishop of Liverpool, Dr Clifford Martin, told those gathered as he dedicated the memorial: 'Some of those who are buried in this great grave are unknown in name but in the dark days of 1941 they were our neighbours.'

Lord Mayor Alderman Reverend H. D. Longbottom said: 'This is a day of very precious but sad memories. None of us can look back upon those war years without feeling that the calamity of the Blitz brought us nearer to each other. It would be a great thing if today we could recall the best of those tragic years.'

A member of the Liverpool City Police Band played *The Last Post* and the following day a separate Roman Catholic service was conducted by the Archbishop of Liverpool. The memorial contains the inscription: 'Erected by the citizens of Liverpool to the memory of all those who gave their lives during the attacks from the air upon the city, of whom 554 are buried in this communal grave. 1939-45.'

MAY 8TH

1915: Desperate crowds gathered in Liverpool seeking news of survivors from the Cunard liner *Lusitania*, which was sunk off the coast of Ireland by a German U-boat the previous day. When the liner left New York on 1 May, Cunard was confident that her speed meant she could escape any submarines. However, at 2.20 p.m. on the 7th she sank in just eighteen minutes after being hit by a torpedo, killing 1,195 of the 1,959 passengers and crew on board.

On 10 May the *Liverpool Daily Courier* called it 'an act of German piracy' and described the scene at Lime Street: 'Friends and relatives of the crew waited hour after hour to greet survivors to arrive and perhaps learn something of the fate of those who were not amongst the incomers'. Relatives also waited anxiously near the Cunard offices: 'In Rumford Street, where posters detailing names were displayed, crowds of men and women, many of the latter with babies of tender years in their arms, stood or sat on the parapet hoping for good news but fearing bad.'

Over 100 Americans were killed, turning public opinion there against Germany. The USA resisted the temptation to enter into the war at that stage, eventually doing so in 1917.

MAY 9TH

1966: The feared traffic chaos failed to materialise after the introduction of a one-way traffic system in many of Liverpool's city centre streets.

The scheme and its consequences had been publicised for many weeks and after it had a low key introduction on the Sunday plenty of officials and police were on hand to help overcome any problems on this Monday morning.

However despite the warnings from doom mongers, things ran smoothly as that evening's *Liverpool Echo* reported: 'A small army of policemen were on duty at vantage points to offer advice where necessary but on the whole motorists seemed to know what they were doing.'

Officials from the City Engineer's Department were described as delighted with the results, although critics claimed that the reasons for things going well were simply that many commuters had played it safe and left their cars at home. Both the AA and RAC welcomed the publicity that had been given in the run in and only two motorists were observed going the wrong direction down one-way streets.

MAY 10TH

1986: Fans of Liverpool and Everton travelled to Wembley together for the FA Cup final. The city's two clubs were dominant in the mid-1980s, when the league championship trophy was won by one or the other for seven successive years. They had already met at Wembley in the League Cup final and Charity Shield in previous years when fans were side by side, but the world's greatest knockout competition was a whole new ball game. Sixteen trains and 400 coaches took fans to Wembley, the *Liverpool Echo* reporting on 12 May: 'How marvellous to see red and blue sitting side by side in the same coach or car, to see blue flags waving in the middle of the Kopites, to see red banners held high surrounded by Howie's army.'

Such a show of unity was a boost for the city after years of negative publicity, culminating a year earlier when thirty-nine Juventus fans died when a wall collapsed after clashes with Liverpool fans at the European Cup final in Brussels. Liverpool won the game 3-1 to complete a double, having already secured the league championship. The following year it was Everton's turn as they pipped the Reds to the title but the clubs haven't been so successful since.

MAY 11TH

1880: A Royal Charter was granted giving Liverpool city status. The charter came about due to Liverpool becoming a diocese, meaning it automatically got city status. It decreed:

That under and by virtue of an Act of Parliament passed on the 16th day of August in the 42nd year of Our reign and intituled an act to provide for the formation of four new bishoprics in England the ecclesiastical commissioners have certified to us under their common seal that the Endowment Fund required by the said Act for the foundation of the Bishopric of Liverpool has been provided that the memorialists prayed if it should please us by order to council to found the said Bishopric that Our Royal Letters Patent authorising the change in the name and denomination of the said Body Corporate and conferring upon Liverpool the title of 'City'. The memorialists shall hereafter be called and known as the 'Mayor Aldermen' and 'Citizens of the City of Liverpool'. Now therefore know ye that we of our especial grace and favour and mere motion do by this Our Royal Charter will ordain constitute declare and appoint that our said Borough of Liverpool shall henceforth for the future and forever hereafter be a City and styled 'The City of Liverpool in the County of Lancaster'. Witness Ourself at Our Palace of Westminster the Eleventh day of May in the forty third year of Our Reign (1880). By Her Majesty's Command.

MAY 12TH

1902: There was mystery surrounding a large sum of cash that was found near to the River Mersey. The *Liverpool Daily Courier* reported the following day:

A remarkable discovery was made by the landing stage yesterday morning. About nine o' clock a passer-by noticed something stuck in the mud by number two bridge. A Seacombe ferry boat hand was informed and he at once proceeded to recover the object, which turned out to be a cash box. It was at once taken possession of by a constable and conveyed to the Central Detective Offices, Dale Street, whereupon being opened it was found to contain bank notes and securities for a large amount. The former was stated to be of the value of £150, while it is further asserted that the securities represented a value of about £8,000. The find is supposed to be the proceeds of a robbery and the thief or thieves got rid of it by throwing it into the water as the best means of disposing of it. There is however some mystery attached to the discovery inasmuch as the police authorities are without information as to the owner of the cashbox and valuables and are further handicapped by the fact that no articles of this character have been notified as being lost.

MAY 13TH

1957: A memorial service was conducted at Liverpool Cathedral for its first Dean, Dr F. W. Dwelly. Dean Dwelly had become Dean on the consecration of the cathedral in 1924, and 2,000 people attended the memorial service, including Deputy Lord Mayor Alderman Reginald Batley. The *Liverpool Echo* reported that evening:

> The full cathedral choir led a procession of clergy and cathedral and diocesan officials into the chancel. This great procession took five minutes to pass. The service was simple without any address. The thanksgiving was led by Revd R.S. Dawson, chaplain of St Edward's church, Cambridge. The Bishop of Liverpool made the blessing.

Dr Dwelly's coffin had been draped in a red and gold cathedral pall and the *Echo* described its final passage:

> The *Nunc Dimittis* faded into a silence as the coffin passed between the choir stalls. Then as the procession reformed and the coffin was borne slowly down the nave the cathedral organ burst into Chopin's *Funeral March*. Out through the main entrance and down the steps with the great bell of the vestry tolling over it, the body of Dean Dwelly went from the cathedral for the last time.

Dean Dwelly was cremated and his ashes interred in the cathedral sanctuary.

MAY 14TH

1967: Liverpool Metropolitan Cathedral was consecrated. Building of the city's Catholic cathedral had begun as recently as 1962, a much grander design having been abandoned due to the Second World War.

It was consecrated on the Feast of Pentecost with 3,000 people present, including three cardinals, Prime Minister Harold Wilson, opposition leader Edward Heath and Irish Prime Minister Jack Lynch.

The following day's *Daily Post* called it a 'brilliant and colourful gathering' due to the 'vivid blue light from the windows contrasting with the brilliant garb of the clerics'. Speaking of the buildings modern design, Papal Legate Cardinal Heenan told those gathered: 'It will be admired as long as men cherish beauty. On this building the architect has spoken in a new language. Though modern this language is not disfigured by tricks and devices to embarrass those who will come later.'

The cathedral's capacity has now been reduced to 2,000, whilst the purchase of surrounding buildings since the Millennium have allowed for steps leading to it forming a much grander entrance.

MAY 15TH

1985: Everton won the European Cup Winners' Cup, adding to the league title they had already secured. In the semi-final Everton had come from behind to beat German giants Bayern Munich to secure a place in their first European final, where they faced Austrian side Rapid Vienna in Rotterdam. The result was rarely in doubt. After a steady first half, Everton gained momentum in the second and cruised to a 3-1 victory thanks to goals from Andy Gray, Trevor Steven and Kevin Sheedy.

The following evening's *Liverpool Echo* had high praise for Everton's fans, who outnumbered the Rapid contingent by at least three to one. They reported:

> The vast blue and white army drank the city dry before the match but still upheld the name of the club that they adore. During the match they turned the beautiful Feyenoord Stadium into a cauldron of noise and colour. Andy Gray's opening goal in the second half marked the start of some amazing scenes of celebration.

Three days later Everton failed to complete an unprecedented treble when they were beaten 1-0 in the FA Cup final by Manchester United.

MAY 16TH

1835: Poet Felicia Dorothea Hemans, author of *Landing of the Pilgrim Fathers* and *Casabianca*, died in Dublin. Hemans was born in Duke Street in 1793 and grew up in North Wales. In 1808 she published her first volume of poetry in Liverpool, but it was her 1826 poem *Casabianca*, containing the line 'the boy stood on the burning deck' and *Landing of the Pilgrim Fathers*, often used to teach American children about Thanksgiving, for which she is best known. She returned to Liverpool in 1828, living in Wavertree High Street before moving to Dublin in 1831. After she died of dropsy the *Liverpool Times* paid tribute to her when announcing her death in the paper on 26 May: 'On Saturday 16th last at Dawson Street, Dublin after a long and painful illness, which she bore with that cheerfulness and pious resignation which was to have been expected from her writings and her character, Mrs Hemans.'

MAY 17TH

1887: The Liverpool public attended events at the Liverpool Exhibition, which was celebrating the Golden Jubilee of Queen Victoria. The exhibition had been formally opened the previous day by Princess Louise, but this was the first day that there was a full programme of events across the city. The next day's *Liverpool Mercury* reported:

> The musical programmes were of the varied and agreeable character and performances of these were greatly enjoyed. Mr W. H. Jude gave a recital of the organ in the north transept. The excellent band of the Scots Guards played in the Old Liverpool Castle. The entertainments at the Royal Victoria Theatre were also numerously attended. In the evening the wonderful electric fountains were seen to great advantage, and a display of fireworks added to the attractiveness of the outdoor programme. The exhibits in the various courts continue to obtain the close attention to which their singularly interesting and instructive nature entitles them.

MAY 18TH

1812: Liverpool merchant John Bellingham was hanged at Newgate in London for assassinating Prime Minister Spencer Perceval in the House of Commons.

Born in Huntingdon, Bellingham had come to Liverpool at the beginning of the century, marrying a local girl. He went to Russia in 1804 as an export agent and ended up being imprisoned for five years over a debt. On returning to England he tried to claim compensation from the government but this was refused. On 11 May 1812 he waited in the lobby of the House of Commons and shot Perceval through the heart before calmly sitting down. He was recognised by Liverpool's MP Isaac Gascoyne and detained. The trial was just four days later and Bellingham told the court he would have preferred to have killed the British ambassador to Russia. Some witnesses said he was insane but he himself didn't use this as an argument. He was found guilty and the execution was carried out in public. The *Liverpool Mercury* reported on 22 May that he mounted the scaffold with 'a cheerful countenance' and 'was proceeding about Russia and his family' before being persuaded by the clergyman to pray due to the 'eternity to which he was entering'. In Liverpool, a subscription was arranged to provide for his wife and children.

MAY 19TH

1898: William Gladstone, who was born in Rodney Street and served as prime minister on four occasions, died of heart failure at his home in Hawarden. Gladstone first became a Conservative MP in 1832 at the age of twenty-three, but by the first of his four spells as prime minister in 1868 he had become a Liberal. In all he was prime minister for twelve and a half years in a twenty-six year period, the last of which came between 1892 and 1894 when he was in his eighties. The following day's *Liverpool Mercury* reported that:

> The news did not come as a surprise: for many weeks the heroic old statesman had been patiently awaiting the change that would bring his release from the painful malady that came upon him with advanced age. We may be sure that we shall never look upon his like again. It is no exaggeration to say that taking him all in all he has been without peer in the contemporary world.

In Liverpool flags flew at half-mast and photographs of him were displayed in windows, the *Mercury* commenting: 'Mr Gladstone was one of Liverpool's noblest sons. His death awakened such a widespread feeling of sorrow in Liverpool.'

He was buried in Westminster Abbey. A statue was unveiled of him in 1904 in Liverpool in St John's Gardens.

MAY 20TH

1868: A youth was brought before the courts charged with wilfully damaging stonework at the new Municipal Buildings in Dale Street. A police officer told the court that he had found William Adams, who lived in Tweed Street, Kensington, scratching at the stone work with a knife causing white marks. Officials said that as a result of the damage the stonework had to be rubbed down, at the cost of a shilling. Imposing a fine of ten shillings plus costs, Magistrate Mr Raffles told Adams:

> It is painful to think that in a civilised country like this that handsome public buildings like this should be exposed to the damage done by idle careless people by such acts as that of the defendant. If I find a case in which anybody chips the stone I will inflict the most severe punishment. I believe such wantonness attaches to us as a nation more than any other people. Such things are not done abroad; on the Continent people respect their public buildings.

MAY 21ST

1956: A crowd of 100,000 flocked to Speke Airport to see an air pageant. The display was organised by the Soldiers, Sailors and Airmen's Families Association (SSAFA) and sponsored by the *Liverpool Echo*. To ensure everyone arrived on time, bus company officials monitored all routes serving the airport and called in extra vehicles as required. Before the display began, the hangars were open so members of the public could see the planes at close quarters.

Of the display itself, which had a commentary provided by Kenneth Wolstenholme, the *Echo* said 'jet planes rendezvous at points 20 miles from Speke then fly in and perform the acrobatics'. Two highlights were the French birdman Leo Valentin, who 'fell like a stone without pulling his ripcord for over 8,000 feet', and a backwards-flying helicopter. Crowds also saw a flypast by eight jets from the Manchester Vampire Squadron and a 250mph take off by a mini-jet. Afterwards SSAFA said: 'We had never organised a more successful air display than today. The public are supporting it in force and the pilots are doing a great job up there.'

MAY 22ND

1876: Two men appeared in court charged with carrying out a robbery in the Saddle public house in Dale Street. The following day's *Liverpool Daily Courier* reported:

> Robert Roberts and James Davies were charged with stealing several bottles of wine, brandy and a table cloth and spoon, the property of Mr J.S. Shaw, the landlord of the Saddle Hotel. The value of the property was £8 14*s*, the brandy being reported to be over 100 years old and worth 22*s* a bottle.

The robbery was something of an 'inside job', as Davies was a night porter at the hotel and Roberts a former boot cleaner there. The court was told how Roberts was arrested for being drunk and incapable at 5.30 a.m. and found to be in possession of the tablecloth and spoon marked as belonging to the Saddle, as well as bottles of wine and sherry. When police went to the hotel and questioned Davies, he confessed that Roberts had shown him how to access the cellar through a fanlight. Police found more bottles in a box which Davies admitted he had also intended to take. Both men were sentenced to three months' imprisonment.

MAY 23RD

1962: Travel between Liverpool and the Isle of Man took a major step forward with the first sailing of the *Manx Maid*, the Isle of Man Steam Packet Co.'s first car ferry. Although cars had been carried on previous ferries, they had to be loaded on and off by crane, a long process that was also dependent on tides. Now for the first time drivers could simply drive down the ramps on arrival, irrespective of the tide; the captain described it as like driving into a car park. The *Manx Maid* was built at Cammel Laird at the cost of over £1 million and could carry up to 1,400 passengers and ninety cars. The next day's *Daily Post* said, of her maiden voyage:

> Motorists began arriving in Liverpool early from many parts of the country and were soon streaming down the floating roadway to the car ferry. They drove straight onto the ship up a metal ramp and onto a turntable, operated by the crew, and then onto the two lanes of the car deck.

On arrival at Douglas: 'The 53 cars and eight motor cycles were driven off in twenty minutes and motorists praised the speed.'
The *Manx Maid* remained in service until 1984.

MAY 24TH

1935: The Lord Mayor visited some city schools as Empire Day was celebrated. First observed in 1902, Empire Day was a celebration of the British Empire, involving maypole dancing, pageants and patriotic singing. Alderman F.T. Richardson visited Clint Road School, where he was a pupil, before going on to Birchfield Road School where a pageant was taking place in the playground. That evening's *Evening Express* reported how he told pupils at Clint Road: 'The British Empire stands for happiness and freedom. When you grow older you will realise that it is only in the British Empire that you get real freedom.' Of the pageant at Birchfield Road, the *Evening Express* said: 'The civic guests were escorted to the playground by boy scouts, girl guides, cubs, brownies and members of the Boys Brigade. A boy scout unveiled a Union Jack which the whole school, numbering about 1,200 scholars, saluted.'

With the decline of the British Empire after the Second World War, Empire Day soon became a thing of the past.

MAY 25TH

1971: Commuters on the Mersey ferries had to do a double take as they saw a 60-ton army tank crossing the river. That evening's *Liverpool Echo* reported that the tank, belonging to the 1st Royal Tank Regiment at Catterick, began its journey at Alfred Dock in Birkenhead on board a special tank transporter on its way to being christened at St George's Plateau. Due to the regiment's links with the city it was being named *Liverpool*. With the Mersey being choppy, the *Echo* reported how Miss Liverpool, nineteen-year-old Tricia O'Donnell, was 'keeping the crews spirits up in the face of a strong gale' and that her red trouser suit and brown floppy hat 'brought a touch of glamour to an otherwise khaki scene'. The tanks stayed on display for a week in Coronation Gardens, off Paradise Street, before taking up operational duties.

MAY 26TH

1977: Seven hundred and fifty thousand people lined the streets to welcome Liverpool FC after their European Cup triumph. The Reds had beaten Borussia Mönchengladbach 3-1 in Rome the previous evening to become European champions for the first time. The victory parade would take them from the airport down Mather Avenue, along Queens Drive, up Utting Avenue to Anfield and then down Scotland Road to the city centre. Describing the homecoming as 'the greatest sporting reception this country has ever seen', the *Daily Post* reported on 27 May: 'Every inch of the 11 mile route was covered in red: they were on the trees, up the traffic lights, on the bus shelters.'

Around 300,000 people were in the area around William Brown Street and St George's Hall, where players were introduced to the crowd in turn. They had been to homecomings before but none on the scale of this one. Steve Heighway described it as 'just magnificent', while keeper Ray Clemence said: 'We keep coming back to these receptions wondering just how many more people will turn out and see us. Today tops the lot.' Ironically, several thousand fans who had been in Rome for the game didn't witness the homecoming as the scheduled trains weren't due to arrive home until the next night.

MAY 27TH

1833: Liverpool Zoological Gardens opened. They were developed by Thomas Atkins, the owner of a travelling menagerie who purchased ten acres of land off West Derby Road from Liverpool Corporation for £2,000. Open from 7 a.m. to dusk, entrance cost 1s and visitors were able to see zebras, big cats, bears, monkeys and aviaries. Although the lions and tigers were caged, gentler animals such as llama and antelope were allowed to roam free. The next day's *Liverpool Times* reported: 'During the last few days several caravans of wild beasts and foreign animals have arrived. We congratulate our townsmen and townswomen on the new source of enjoyment open to them and to wish Mr Atkins the success which his spirit, enterprise and good taste so richly merit.'

The zoo would only be open for twenty years before it went bankrupt. The next zoo to open in Liverpool was off Rice Lane in Walton in 1884, but this again barely lasted twenty years.

MAY 28TH

1949: The liner *Caledonia* delayed its sailing for half an hour at the request of a late passenger who still failed to show – which proved good fortune for another passenger held up by customs. The *Daily Post* reported on 30 May:

> *Caledonia* was held back for half an hour on Saturday for a man who telephoned that he had missed his train at London. The liner however sailed for Bombay without him, having waited for a later London train which the intending passenger also apparently missed. The delay was fortunate for another passenger, a representative in India, Pakistan and Burma for British knitwear firms. He was returning with two large cardboard boxes of samples to show Britain's latest designs and the wrong invoices turned up at the Customs. As a result of the delay he was able to rush on board and find documents sufficient to clear his samples and a minute later the *Caledonia* sailed.

MAY 29TH

1832: Liverpool saw the first of several incidents of cholera riots which took place that summer. The disease of cholera brought symptoms of vomiting, diarrhoea and dehydration and could lead to death. At the time it was not known how it was caused or spread. The riots were borne out of suspicion of the medical profession: cholera sufferers, it was thought, were being killed unnecessarily by doctors so bodies could be sold for anatomical research. Four years earlier two Irish immigrants in Edinburgh, Burke and Hare, had been hanged for a series of murders where their victim's bodies were sold for research.

The riots began at the Liverpool Cholera Hospital in Toxteth Park, where a man and wife from Derbyshire had admitted themselves voluntarily. A letter written by a doctor published in *Gore's General Advertiser* on 31 May said: 'The mob were shouting they were to be cut up, the surgeons were the getters up, there is no such thing as cholera in the town. They finished by breaking the windows of the hospital, gentlemen of the committee of health were on the spot and struck with stones, brickbats etc.' The riots went on throughout the city until 10 June and ended after appeals from local churchmen.

MAY 30TH

1889: The body of Aigburth merchant James Maybrick was exhumed from its grave at Anfield Cemetery as mystery surrounding his death deepened.

Maybrick had died on 11 May and his wife, Florence, was arrested on the 14th and charged with murder, based on evidence provided by servants and Maybrick's brothers that Florence had purchased arsenic. On 28 May an inquest opened, and the coroner ordered an exhumation of the body. The *Liverpool Mercury* reported the exhumation on 1 June:

> A couple of garden seats were pulled up to the graveside and upon these rested the coffin. The lid was quickly lifted, the linen shroud torn clear from the corpse and in a moment the sharp blade of steel deftly directed by Dr Barron had passed down the centre of the body. The lungs, heart, kidneys were removed and a moment later the scalp plate had been cleared and the brain extracted. All the organs named were placed in a stone jar. The coffin lid was again screwed down and the body, or rather all that remained of the remains of James Maybrick, was lowered into the grave.

Florence was later found guilty of murder and sentenced to death, but her sentence was later commuted to life imprisonment, of which she served fifteen years.

MAY 31ST

1982: Pope John Paul II left Liverpool to continue his British tour after a memorable visit to the city. The Pope had arrived the previous afternoon, a Sunday, to be greeted by a crowd of 150,000 at Speke Airport, where a special Mass had been held. Hundreds of thousands lined the streets as he travelled in the 'Popemobile' to the Anglican Cathedral where he said the Lord's Prayer, before he moved on to the Metropolitan Cathedral to celebrate Mass with Archbishop Derek Worlock. After Mass he went on a walkabout amongst crowds, who had waited in glorious sunshine, and then spent the night at Archbishop Worlock's Woolton home.

On the morning of the 31st there were more crowds at Speke as he boarded a helicopter for Manchester, beginning a hectic day that would also take him to York and Edinburgh. The following day's *Daily Post* reported of his departure: 'The Pope gave a special thank you gift when he left the city yesterday. As he said farewell to civic dignitaries at Speke Airport, Pope John Paul pressed a Papal medallion into the hand of Lord Mayor Stanley Airey. It was a gift for the city of Liverpool.' Pope John Paul II remains the only Pope to have visited Liverpool.

JUNE IST

1950: The first passenger helicopter service in the world started between Liverpool, Wrexham and Cardiff. The route was developed by British European Airways and operated three times a day, with return fares between Liverpool and Cardiff costing £5 10s and helicopters being able to carry three passengers per journey.

The first flight carried government minister Lord Pakenham and Lord Douglas, chairman of British European Airways. That evening's *Evening Express* reported: 'Air history was made today by the start of the world's first scheduled passenger helicopter service. Perfectly to schedule the first helicopter rose from the grass at Speke Airport at 9.15 a.m.' After a 22-minute flight to Wrexham the helicopter was met by civic dignitaries and the town's Mayor joined the flight to Cardiff, where it arrived two minutes behind schedule at 11.37 a.m., but making a perfect landing.

The route did not prove to be a success and was ended after a year, the airline's belief that scheduled helicopters would be the future of air travel not coming to fruition.

JUNE 2ND

1903: Two foreign sailors were hanged for the murder of their captain in the first double execution at Walton Gaol.

The previous December five sailors who claimed to have been shipwrecked after a fire were picked up by a British freighter off the coast of Brazil. Suspicions arose when it was noticed one was particularly nervous of the others and Gustav Rau, a German, was wearing the captain's clothing. All five were handed over to the police on arrival in Liverpool and it transpired that the captain, Alexander McLeod, had been killed – along with six other crew members of the crew. Following a trial, Rau, another German, Otto Monson, and Dutchman Willem Schmidt were found guilty of murder and sentenced to hang. Monson was reprieved due to his young age but Rau and Schmidt went to the gallows on 2 June, Rau's last words being: 'I am not guilty of the murder of these men'.

The following day's *Liverpool Mercury* reported: 'The awful story of mutiny and murder sent a thrill of horror throughout the civilised world. Not the slightest sympathy was extended to the two ringleaders by the general public. Both men awaited their end with much the same stolid indifference as had marked their bearing during the trial.'

JUNE 3RD

1969: There was good news for residents in Broadgreen when it was confirmed their new homes would not have to be demolished to make way for the M62 motorway. Liverpool Corporation flats in The Green had only been built four years earlier, but there were concerns that they were in line with the proposed motorway and Queens Drive flyover. That evening's *Liverpool Echo* carried a quote from a spokesman of the traffic route engineering section who explained the situation: 'If the motorway goes through as proposed these flats won't be affected physically. There will be a flyover carrying Queens Drive but we feel, and so does the housing department, that it is far enough away from the flats.'

However, there were still concerns raised by Roger Johnston of the Wavertree Liberal Party, who said: 'I hope the Corporation will consider putting in double glazing on these flats, occupied mostly by retired elderly people, to cut down the noise from the proposed motorway. This should be a necessity.' As it was the M62 terminated at Queens Drive, with junctions one, two and three never being completed.

JUNE 4TH

2003: It was announced that Liverpool was to be Capital of Culture for 2008. The city beat off strong competition from Birmingham and Newcastle/Gateshead to secure the nomination, which was announced by Culture Secretary Tessa Jowell at 8.10 a.m. The announcement was greeted with scenes of jubilation at the Empire Theatre, where the bid team had gathered, and across the city with car horns sounding during the rush hour. Liverpool City Council leader Mike Storey likened the news to Liverpool winning the Champions League, Everton the double and The Beatles reforming all on the same day. That evening the *Liverpool Echo* reported:

> Tessa Jowell headed straight to Liverpool after making the announcement and was taken on a tour to see for herself what made the twelve judges choose our bid. Jowell was arriving at Lime Street with Chairman of the judges Sir Jeremy Isaacs. Schoolchildren with home-made placards were there to greet them along with a military band.

The culture year of 2008 was a huge success and the *Guardian* estimated that 7,000 events had been staged, involving 10,000 artists – with £4 billion of investment being attracted to the city – since the 2003 announcement.

JUNE 5TH

1919: A large-scale disturbance occurred between Jamaican and Scandinavian sailors in Great George Square, leaving one Jamaican dead and four policemen wounded. The following day's *Daily Post and Mercury*, referring to it as a feud that culminated in a disastrous encounter, reported:

> The disturbance began at the corner of Bailey Street and Grenville Street. A number of coloured men quarrelled with several Swedes and words led to a fight in which the Negroes drew knives and razors. A constable interfered and was badly slashed about the face and back and fell exhausted to the ground.

When more police arrived on the scene, shots were fired from the Jamaicans' lodgings in Upper Pitt Street, one bullet passing through the mouth of a constable into his sergeant behind. Another policeman broke his wrist trying to restore order. A large crowd had gathered, the paper reporting: 'A Negro suspected of firing a revolver ran away towards the dockside and was followed by a hostile crowd, a number of policemen joining in the pursuit. The fugitive went straight to the Queens Dock and here he either jumped into the water or was thrown into the dock by the angry crowd. He was drowned and eventually his body was recovered.'

One of the injured policemen was detained at hospital, whilst police made several arrests later that evening.

JUNE 6TH

1937: An estimated 2,000 people attended a memorial service in Edge Hill for two railway workers who had died following an accident – but not before they had ensured the safety of all passengers. Driver Joseph Ball and fireman Cormack Higgins were on the Euston-Liverpool train on 20 May when a smoke-box deflector plate fault caused the cab to catch fire near Primrose Hill. Both managed to bring the train to a stop in a safe place but were so badly burned they died from their injuries in hospital.

On 7 June the *Daily Post* wrote of the service that was held at St Mary's church:

> Tributes were paid yesterday to the memory and bravery of the two Liverpool LMS railwaymen. Over 500 railwaymen and workmates marched in procession to the church, headed by their band. They and 400 members of the public filled the church. The others followed the service by means of an outside relay by loudspeakers. The vicar, in tribute to the men, said he felt far too little tribute had been accorded them – 'I feel the public realises all too little what immense risks and sacrifices must be made day after day in order that the public services may be maintained.'

A commemorative plaque to the two men is situated on platform one at Lime Street Station.

JUNE 7TH

1872: The Mariners' church, situated on a converted ship in George's Dock, sank. Formerly the HMS *Tees*, the vessel was presented to the Mariners' Church Society in 1827 as a church for seamen. She was in a considerable state of disrepair when she sank in the early hours of the morning. The disaster was believed to have been caused by rats gnawing away at timbers in the hull.

The *Liverpool Mercury* broke the news briefly on 7 June, reporting that a watchman raised the alarm but despite the dock master's strenuous efforts, she couldn't be saved. The news caused quite a stir, the *Mercury* reporting on 8th: 'The sinking of the Mariners' floating church in George's Dock aroused considerable interest throughout the town and in the course of the day the place was visited by thousands of persons.' The dock wasn't deep, meaning some salvage was possible: 'The water only raised to the backs of the seats in the body of the church, so that the organ was fortunately preserved from serious injury. It was yesterday afternoon removed by Messrs Rushworth and Sons, the organ builders, of Islington.'

Now sailors had no dedicated church, so St Nicholas became unofficially known as the 'sailor's church' instead.

JUNE 8TH

1827: Thomas Littledale, Lord Mayor of Liverpool, laid the first stone as construction commenced on New Brighton Lighthouse. The lighthouse was built to replace a wooden perch to which a light was attached to navigate shipping, but was often washed away. Of the ceremony, the *Liverpool Mercury* on 15 June reported: 'The Mayor was joined by several of the members of the Common Council and 100 to 150 of the leading merchants and most respectable inhabitants of the town.' After being given a silver trowel by architect John Foster, the Mayor spread mortar on a stone before laying it into place and saying to those present: 'May the blessing of God attend this undertaking. May it be the means of saving the lives of the seamen of England and also those from other countries who may visit our shores.'

The lighthouse, which was 90ft tall, was completed in 1830 and could be seen 14 miles away. Modern technology meant that the lighthouse ceased to be used in 1973 and was bought by a local businessman, who for a short time offered it to couples as a honeymoon suite.

JUNE 9TH

1856: Toxteth Park Cemetery was consecrated by the Bishop of Chester. The cemetery, which covered 30 acres and had two chapels and lodges, cost a total of £26,000 to prepare, of which £15,000 was needed to buy the land. The *Daily Post* reported:

> The ceremony of consecration had been fixed to commence at eleven o'clock and notwithstanding the threatening state of the weather a large concourse of ladies and gentlemen were present at the hours, within a few minutes of which the Lord Bishop drove up to the gate, where he was received by the contractors, the members of the burial board, the members of the Town Council, and others, who moved from the lodge to the chapel. The procession marched to the chapel where the rites prescribed for the consecration for such and edifice and such were duly observed and gone through by the Bishop. His Lordship, together with some of the leading clergy and Deputy-Mayor, signed the deed of consecration and as far as they were concerned the services of the day were at an end.

The first internment took place on 17 June and the cemetery is still being used for burials today.

JUNE 10TH

1920: Liverpool's fruit traders enjoyed their annual day out in North Wales. The following day's *Liverpool Daily Courier* reported:

> The members of the Liverpool fruit trade and their friends had a most enjoyable day on the occasion of their annual picnic. A large party of about 240 persons travelled by motor charabanc from Birkenhead to Halkyn (Flint) where lunch was served under canvas in the most delightful surroundings. The party then proceeded under the direction of guides over the wildest part of Flint Mountain and eventually arrived at Denbigh. From Denbigh the party returned to Halkyn by the Holyhead road and tea was followed by dancing on the green. The glorious weather contributed most to the day's success.

JUNE 11TH

1644: Arrangements were made to pay compensation to the families of soldiers slain by Prince Rupert's troops as Liverpool was re-taken by Royalists during the English Civil War. The previous day Rupert had taken Liverpool to secure the port; he planned to bring in more re-enforcements from Ireland. Most of the Parliamentary garrison had sailed away as Rupert stormed the town, but around 400 soldiers were left behind. They were butchered. Sir Edward Moore signed documents accounting for what relief money had been paid out, stating:

> These are to signify unto whom it shall or may be pleased to take into consideration what money the distressed cause of the poor widows of Liverpool that had their husbands or children slain by Prince Rupert's soldiers and to certify what money they had received towards their relief.

A total of fifty-four residents received money, with two examples being:

Anne Rose – Had her husband slain by Prince Rupert's soldiers, left with four children of her son Edward Tatlock that was slain by Prince Rupert's soldiers and ye mother dead. £1 6s 0d.

William Worrall – lamed utterly by Prince Rupert's soldiers so that he cannot dress or feed himself. 9s.

JUNE 12TH

1907: The Bowring Park estate opened to the public. Formerly the Roby Hall Estate, it was offered to Liverpool Council after being purchased in 1906 by Alderman William Benjamin Bowring, on the condition that it was used for the benefit of the city's inhabitants. In recognition of Bowring's gift, the estate was re-named the Bowring Estate and formally handed over at a ceremony on Wednesday 12 June, an unusually stormy day for the time of year. The following day's *Liverpool Daily Courier* reported:

> A pleasant social function over which the Lord Mayor presided marked the proceedings. Mr Bowring was warmly thanked for his magnificent gift and was presented by the Lord Mayor on behalf of the Corporation with a silver gilt casket containing a bound copy of the day's proceedings and a vote of thanks of the City Council.

The estate has since seen an eighteen-hole golf course developed on it, as well as some housing development. It has also been split in two by the M62 motorway.

JUNE 13TH

1876: The Presbyterian Church of England was formed at the Philharmonic Hall when the United Presbyterian Church merged with the English Presbyterian Church. The following day's *Liverpool Mercury* described the gathering as 'immense and impressive', reporting:

> Both synods proceeded to form themselves into processional order and march to the Philharmonic Hall. It had been arranged by the local committee of management that the two synods should meet for the first time at the door of the Philharmonic Hall in Myrtle Street. At a quarter to twelve the two streams met and mingling together, passed into the hall in profound silence – it being impossible to distinguish one form of Presbyterians from the other. After the preliminaries had been disposed of the declaration of union was made by Mr Rankine and subsequently with a few verbal exchanges by Dr Dykes. The members of the two uniting churches stood up and at the close each gave to the other the right hand of fellowship.

In 1972 the Presbyterian Church of England merged with the Congregational Church of England and Wales to form the United Reform Church.

JUNE 14TH

1985: Liverpool City Council set an illegal budget, putting itself on a collision course with Central Government. The Militant Labour Council had maintained that they had no choice but to set a budget beyond the limits imposed by the Conservative government due to the city's housing, educational and recreational needs. The following day's *Daily Post* reported that leader John Hamilton, who acknowledged he may go to jail, told the chamber:

> If we go down and are defeated in legal terms, in terms of decent humanity we will win. We talk in a cool language of figures and statistics for what is required for the city, but at the end of the day these cold statistics are human life. We say we need this money to regenerate this area, to provide jobs and services.

The next few months were tense, with 30,000 council workers receiving redundancy notices as the city faced bankruptcy. Eventually a £30 million loan was secured from Swiss banks to balance the books in what was termed an 'orderly retreat'. Although the new sports centres, houses and parks were developed, the militant councillors were expelled from the Labour Party and disqualified from holding office.

JUNE 15TH

1967: There were tearful scenes at Lime Street Station as twenty-eight Jewish volunteers set off for Israel. In the aftermath of the Six Day War, which had ended five days earlier, many Jews from all over the world were heading to Israel to show solidarity. The volunteers were expected to work in all aspects of the collective community of kibbutz life and that evening's *Liverpool Echo* reported how they had been told by Councillor Ben Shaw: 'That it will be no picnic. They will be asked to undertake all types of work, probably in the pioneering settlements along the borders and in Sinai and Galilee.'

On the departure of the train to London, the *Echo* described how 'women dabbed the tears from their eyes as the train pulled out of the station'. Alderman Louis Cain paid tribute to the volunteers, saying: 'We are very proud of the spirit and enthusiasm of the Jewish youngsters in Liverpool who are volunteering for this.'

JUNE 16TH

1934: Shoppers in Church Street had a surprise after a cuckoo clock was installed. The clock was placed above the premises of Schierwater & Lloyd Ltd, watchmakers and jewellers. The *Evening Express* reported that later:

> Tramcar drivers looked puzzled, motorists scratched their heads and pedestrians stopped and listened. Unmistakably above the noise of the traffic came the familiar call – cuckoo, cuckoo. The bird had not strayed from the countryside but forms part of an interesting cuckoo clock which has been installed above the premises of Messrs Schierwater and Lloyd Ltd. The clock is a 24 hour all-electric one which is illuminated at night. There is also a small floodlight which automatically brings the cuckoo into the limelight when it appears from its nest every hour and calls the hour. This is the only clock of its type in the world and hundreds of people waited in Church Street as each hour approached to hear the cuckoo's call.

JUNE 17TH

1957: Liverpool's 750th birthday celebrations began. The following day, the *Daily Post* reported how the Lord Mayor Alderman Frank H. Cain, dressed in full regalia despite temperatures soaring into the eighties, spent a busy day opening events connected to the city's history, industry and maritime heritage. He also watched a guard mounting ceremony, entertained members of the Charter Committee for lunch and listened to a recital on the restored organ at St George's Hall. The day rounded off with a supper dance for city councillors at the Town Hall that ended at 1 a.m.

He told the *Daily Post*: 'This has certainly been my busiest ever day, but it has also been one of the most delightful of my life. Everyone has worked very loyally for the sake of the Charter celebrations and I feel very proud of the city.'

The events went on for two more weeks. By the time the next major anniversary came around in 2007, the celebrations were not as high profile as may have been expected due to the Capital of Culture taking place the following year.

JUNE 18TH

1857: Farming ties between Speke and other districts of South West Lancashire and Cheshire were strengthened when they hosted an exchange visit. The visit was arranged by James Langshaw of Woodend Farm, and the following day's *Liverpool Mercury* reported: 'Upon arriving at Speke Station the visitors were conducted to the residence of Mr James Langshaw, about a quarter of a mile from the station, where they sat down to a sumptuous breakfast, ably presided over by Mrs James Langshaw, the kind hearted hostess.'

The guests had a look at Mr Langshaw's 100 acre farm, where he grew wheat and potatoes, before moving on to Mr Atherton's farm, where they had lunch and inspected his potatoes, turnips and cattle. Next stop was Speke Hall, where the *Mercury* reported that Mr Watt had laid on a spread of 'wine, ale, bread and cheese'. After being shown around the hall and grounds they inspected Mr Cartwright's farm, where he grew barley, potatoes and turnips. After dinner with Mr and Mrs Cartwright, several toasts were proposed and the *Mercury* quoted Mathias Tasker of Upholland as having told the paper: 'He hoped it would not be long before a return visit was got up on the Wigan side. He had learned and seen what he never could forget viz. splendid farming.'

JUNE 19TH

1864: The Confederate raider *Alabama* was sunk off the coast of northern France, having captured sixty-five Union ships during the last two years.

The *Alabama* was built at Cammell Laird and funded by Liverpool Confederates sympathisers and agents. However, as Britain was neutral in the American Civil War she was officially launched as a merchant ship, the *Enrica*, before being fitted out for war off the Azores. Over the next two years she sought out Union shipping in the Atlantic, Gulf of Mexico and Indian Ocean, never entering a Southern port. She was finally sunk by the Federal Steamer *Kearsage* at the Battle of Cherbourg, having cost the Unionists $6 million in losses, leading to a claim against the British government. The following day's *Liverpool Daily Courier* reported:

> At half past twelve the *Alabama* was in a sinking state. The *Deerhound* made towards her and on passing the *Kearsage* was requested to assist in saving the crew of the *Alabama*. The *Deerhound* lowered her boats and succeeded in saving about forty men.

The wreck of the *Alabama* was discovered in 1984 and many artefacts were recovered in 2002 which are now on display in Washington DC.

June 20th

1819: The SS *Savannah*, the first steamship in the world, arrived in Liverpool from New York. Originally built as a sailing packet in New York, Savannah firm Scarborough and Isaacs purchased the vessel and added a steam engine and paddlewheels. Unfortunately, preparations for the voyage didn't go fully to plan: difficulties were faced recruiting crew, the ship having been dubbed a 'steam coffin' in New York. The day before she was due to set sail one of the crew fell off the gangplank whilst drunk and drowned; nobody thereafter was willing to risk their lives or property on the sailing.

When she left New York on 22 May, it was without passengers or freight and instead was sailing in an experimental capacity. On 25 June the *Liverpool Mercury* briefly reported of its arrival: 'On Sunday last a beautiful steamship arrived here in 26 days. She is called the *Savannah* and was built in New York under the inspection of her commander Captain Rogers.'

It was twenty years before steamships regularly crossed the Atlantic as, although the *Savannah* proved it could be done, the size of its engine left little room for passengers, rendering such a service uneconomical.

JUNE 21ST

1976: A Liverpool teen pop band was denied the chance to appear on BBC television programme *Blue Peter* after the intervention of education authorities.

Our Kid had won ITV's *New Faces* talent show the previous month but were not allowed to appear on *Blue Peter* as they had not requested a licence to do so. That evening's *Liverpool Echo* reported a council spokesman as saying: '21 days notice should be given to the education authority before an appearance. One licence has already been issued for them to take part in their summer season in Great Yarmouth and it was doubtful whether a second could be given to them at the same time.'

Blue Peter presenters blamed 'circumstances beyond our control' for the non-appearance of the band, who had turned up at the studios. The band's spokesman disputed the council's approach, claiming that the boys' education came first and that they were due to start school in Great Yarmouth the next day. There was some consolation for Our Kid when their debut single, 'You Just Might See Me Cry', reached number two in the charts but they soon disappeared into obscurity.

JUNE 22ND

1960: Eleven people were killed after a massive fire at Henderson's store on the corner of Church Street and Whitechapel. The shops were usually closed on Wednesday afternoons, but Henderson's was one of the few stores that remained open. The fire was caused by an electrical fault and began at 2.30 p.m., ravaging through the store at an alarming rate. It needed twenty-seven ambulances and one hundred firemen to tackle the blaze and four customers, five staff and two contractors were killed, having been trapped on the fourth floor. The following day's *Daily Post* reported:

> The scene in Church Street resembled the worst days of the blitz, with smoke belching from the store and a tangled jungle of hoses lying in the road. At the height of the fire flames leaped sixty feet across Williamson Street. A vast, lowering pall of black smoke blotted the city centre. While silent crowds watched from surrounding streets stretcher after stretcher, each containing a charred body, was swung from the store and lowered to the street.

The legacy of the fire was the 1963 Office, Shops & Railway Premises Act, which tightened up the rules for escape routes. Henderson's was rebuilt and continued trading under that name until 1975 when it changed to Binns. Various shops now occupy the site.

JUNE 23RD

1883: There was an attack on Allsop's Waxworks in Lime Street, believed to have been carried out by Irish nationalists. Earlier that month, five men had been hanged for the Phoenix Park murders, when Chief Secretary for Ireland, Lord Frederick Cavendish, and his undersecretary, Thomas Henry Burke, were stabbed in Dublin.

On this Saturday night, four men, one of whom was heard to have a strong Irish accent, entered the waxworks and headed for the exhibit depicting the murders. They climbed over the protective rails. The *Liverpool Mercury* reported:

> They set about in earnest to give an imitation of the Phoenix Park tragedy. The figure of Mr Burke, with a long dagger in it, was smashed about the face until it was unrecognisable. That of Lord Frederick Cavendish was demolished in a like manner. Half a dozen policemen arrived on the scene and two of the ruffians were captured and conveyed to the police station.

A third man was also found hiding under some stairs but the fourth escaped. They were charged with wilful damage totalling £200.

JUNE 24TH

1699: Liverpool became a separate parish, having previously been a chapel of ease to Walton-on-the-Hill. Liverpool had first sought to be a parish in 1654, but it did not occur until an Act of Parliament in 1699. In 1833, Thomas Kaye wrote of the Act in his *The Stranger in Liverpool*:

> It was granted that from the twenty-fourth day of that year the town and liberties of Liverpool should be a distinct parish itself, separate from Walton; that the Corporation should have the power to build a new church, and a house for the rector, and to raise the sum of £400, by assessment on the inhabitants, for that purpose: that two rectors should be appointed, one for the new church, the other for the parochial chapel, who should enjoy all ecclesiastical benefits and advantages within the said town and liberties, as the rector and vicar of Walton enjoyed; that all parish dues, contributions, land and houses belonging to the said rector, should be equally divided between the two rectors; that the patronage and presentation to the rectory should be vested in the Mayor, Aldermen and Common Council; and in case, any dispute should arise, the Lord Bishop of Chester should decide and appoint which of the two should be chosen.

This was an unusual move in that Liverpool, with a population of five thousand, would have two parish churches. The old parochial church became the church of St Nicholas, while St Peter's in Church Street opened in 1704 and closed in 1919.

JUNE 25TH

1899: A badly mutilated body was found on the tracks at James Street station. Under the headline 'A GHASTLY DISCOVERY', the following day's *Liverpool Mercury* reported:

At 12.35 a.m. on Sunday morning a foreman platelayer was going his usual rounds when upon emerging from the tunnel he saw the severed pieces of a man's body lying between the rails and the outgoing platform to Birkenhead. The body of the unfortunate man, who had evidently fallen from the platform during the approach of a train, was frightfully lacerated. Both legs had been torn off below the knee while the upper portion of these limbs had been terribly mangled. The right hand had also been torn off. The deceased was dressed in his working clothes and his appearance indicated that he had not been home since leaving work. The mutilated remains were removed to the Prince's mortuary.

The dead man was named as seventy-seven-year-old Frederick Marsden, who worked for wine merchants Rigbys in Dale Street. He was described by the *Mercury* as 'a good character and subject to paralytic strokes'.

JUNE 26TH

1834: The foundation stone was laid for the church of St John the Evangelist in Knotty Ash. A bronze plaque was laid with the plinth stone which read:

> On the 26th day of June Anno Domini, 1834, this Foundation Stone was laid by Adam Dugdale Esq. of Dovecot House, on land given by him for the erection of this church for the service of the Church of England; it is dedicated to St John the Evangelist, and was built by donations and subscriptions.

The church, which celebrated its 175th anniversary in 2011, is adorned with beautiful stained-glass windows. Its graveyard claims to have more Mayors and Lord Mayors of Liverpool buried there than any other in the city.

JUNE 27TH

1971: People were allowed to walk through the new Kingsway tunnel, linking Liverpool with Wallasey.

The second road tunnel under the River Mersey was constructed over a five-year period after it became apparent that the Queensway tunnel, linking Liverpool with Birkenhead, couldn't cope with the volume of traffic. The new tunnel was formally opened three days earlier by Queen Elizabeth II but traffic still hadn't been allowed to pass through it. Pedestrians were charged 25p to walk through the tunnel, which included a return trip on the bus and ferry and were given a certificate at the end. The following day's *Daily Post* reported: 'A human tide flooded Kingsway as 90,000 people took a once in a lifetime walk under the River Mersey yesterday. Local Rotary Club workers, who organised the charity walk, were staggered by the size of the crowds that flocked to stroll through the one and a half mile tunnel.'

Around midnight the first cars were allowed through and in both tunnels tolls were increased from 10p to 15p. The tunnel now carries as many as 50,000 vehicles a day.

JUNE 28TH

1952: A fire occurred at Croxteth Hall, home of the Earl of Sefton. The hall was first built in 1575 and expanded in several stages over the years. The fire began at 5.30 p.m. on a Saturday evening in an unused bedroom and soon spread to the servants' quarters, where the alarm was raised by a chef.

The *Liverpool Echo* reported on 30 June that Lady Sefton had run half a mile from the paddock and Lord Derby came from Knowsley Hall to help: 'Books from the library were recovered by a chain of staff and fire personnel. Valuable pictures, including a Gainsborough, were retrieved and furniture and carpets saved from major damage.'

The morning room, old breakfast room and drawing room were severely damaged and have not been restored since. After the Earl of Sefton died in 1972 with no descendants, the hall passed to Liverpool City Council and is now open to the public and used for functions.

JUNE 29TH

1904: St John's Gardens, to the rear of St George's Hall, were opened. St John's church was demolished in 1898 and the decision was taken to landscape the cemetery, re-interring the bodies elsewhere. The St John's Ornamental and Memorial Gardens, to give them their full name, were designed by City Surveyor Thomas Shelmerdine and contained a Boer War memorial and statues of notable local people. The following day's *Liverpool Daily Courier* commented: 'The people of Liverpool are now in possession of a fine open space, offering greater opportunity for the enjoyment of the fresh air.'

The simple opening ceremony was overseen by Lord Mayor R. Alfred Hampson, who invited chairman of the Joint Committee Alderman Joseph Ball to unlock the gates for the public to enjoy them. Alderman Ball said that he trusted: 'The public would, considering the handsome and artistic way in which the gardens were laid out, respect them and protect them to the best of their ability.'

The gardens remain today a key open space for office workers, shoppers and tourists to escape the bustle of the city centre.

JUNE 30TH

1939: The last ferry service between Liverpool and Rock Ferry sailed after being in operation for more than 200 years.

Passengers on the ferries had been in gradual decline due to the rail tunnels, and for financial reasons the Birkenhead Corporation decided to close its southern terminals. New Ferry closed in 1922 and Eastham in 1929. Rock Ferry's closure would leave Woodside as the only one left in Birkenhead. The *Liverpool Echo* reported on the day:

> The Rock Ferry ferryboat service will be discontinued after tonight, the last boat leaving Liverpool landing stage at 10 p.m. and Rock Ferry pier at 10.20 p.m. Members of the Mersey Tunnel Joint Committee and of the Birkenhead Corporation Ferries Committee are to take part in the final double journey. Thus the River Mersey will lose another ferry service.

Although the terminal building and landing stage have now been demolished, the pier survives as part of the Tranmere oil terminal.

During the 1970s passenger numbers slumped even further with the opening of the second road tunnel leaving the very existence of the ferries under threat. However, they have managed to re-invent themselves for mini-cruises with commuters using them at peak times only.

JULY 1ST

1933: A huge pageant took place as Liverpool Airport was opened by the Secretary of State for Air the Marquis of Londonderry. Flights to Birmingham and London had begun from Speke in 1930 but they only lasted a few months, leading to it operating as a flying club only. However, in 1932 Liverpool Corporation appointed an airport manager and the official opening of what was then the largest civil aerodrome in the country was set for 1 July.

After a drizzly start, the weather turned fine for a twelve-hour display of flying acrobatics, landing competitions and parachuting involving two hundred aircraft and watched by twenty thousand people. That evening's *Evening Express* reported of the opening formalities that the Lord Mayor and Marquis of Londonderry circled in a car to receive the cheers of the crowd before the Marquis said at the declaration: 'This is one more instance of the enterprise of Liverpool and Lancashire and I have great pleasure in declaring the Liverpool Air Port open.'

JULY 2ND

1944: William Rushworth, head of the Rushworth's music firm, died. Rushworth was managing director of the firm, founded by his grandfather in Yorkshire in 1828; the company moved to Liverpool in the late 1800s. Under the headline 'LOSS TO LIVERPOOL MUSICAL LIFE' the next day's *Daily Post* reported: 'Mr Rushworth was at work in his office on Friday afternoon when he collapsed and was taken by his son to the Royal Infirmary, where he died yesterday morning. Mr Rushworth was for many years a public spirited worker for a variety of good causes. In recognition of his public work he was awarded an MBE in 1941.'

Rushworth's remained an institution in the local music scene, selling instruments from their store in Whitechapel until the company went into receivership in 1997.

JULY 3RD

1868: The first concert was given by the Liverpool Police Band. The proposal to form a band was put to the head constable on 15 June and approved immediately, due to the popularity of musicians amongst officers. The concert, which took place at St George's Plateau, was conducted in front of an audience that included twelve VIPs and took place alongside the forces weekly parade, which was moved from its usual venue in Hatton Garden.

The following day's *Liverpool Mercury* reported:

> The band, which until this time has been under the training of Police Constable Beardhall, formerly bandmaster in the army and composed, of course, entirely of men connected with the force, numbered about twelve performers and was stationed in front of the hall. Considering the short time the members of the band have been in practice the performance yesterday was highly creditable. The different pieces were played with marked precision and with a taste which reflected great credit to both teachers and pupils.

The band is still in existence today as the Merseyside Police Band, having performed at the funerals of officers, to royalty and in front of thousands of schoolchildren.

July 4th

1981: The Toxteth Riots began, bringing devastation to the Liverpool 8 area. The previous night police were accused of being heavy-handed when arresting a motorcyclist, leading to a disturbance that saw three policemen injured. At 5.30 p.m. on 4 July an uneasy calm that had existed all day was shattered as disturbances began, followed by full-scale rioting. The *Liverpool Echo* reported on 6 July:

> Youths armed with stones launched an attack on the police and similar hit and run sorties continued until, shortly before midnight, came the incident that was to spark off the full scale riots. A gang of black youths in Upper Parliament Street turned over a workman's generator to use as a barricade. As cars slowed down to pass they came under a hail of stones. A witness said 'black and white youths were running amok. It wasn't a race riot, they were all against the police'. Firemen were forced to stand behind police barricades and watch the rioters set fire to buildings.'

The riots went on for nine days, with police being drafted in from other counties to help quell them. Soon afterwards Michael Heseltine was appointed as Minister for Merseyside and he went on to oversee a number of regeneration schemes in the region.

JULY 5TH

1933: Liverpool's Philharmonic Hall was destroyed by fire. The hall, built in 1849, could seat 2,100 and was described by a *Times* correspondent when it opened as 'one of the finest and best adapted to music that I have ever entered'. The following day the *Manchester Guardian* reported:

> The Liverpool Philharmonic Hall, one of the finest concert halls in England, was destroyed by a fire that broke out early last evening. The caretaker of a neighbouring Unitarian church saw smoke coming from the roof and realising that the building would not be heated in summer, summoned the fire brigade. Almost as soon as the brigade arrived the roof fell in. Sheets of flame were clearly visible from a great distance. Many thousands of people filled the streets and hundreds came from the suburbs and the Wirral to watch the fire. When the roof collapsed several firemen and salvage men had narrow escapes from death. The only casualties were two slight cases of burning. Several treasures inside the building were saved by the salvage men, notably a tablet to the memory of the musicians on the *Titanic*.

The hall was damaged beyond repair and had to be demolished and rebuilt, the new building opening in 1939.

JULY 6TH

1891: American showman Buffalo Bill brought his show to Newsham Park. William Frederick Cody, to give him his full name, earned his title by killing over four thousand buffalo in eighteen months. He toured the USA and Europe with shows that had a Wild West theme.

Two weeks of performances were given at Newsham Park, where a circuit 1 mile long was laid out and four thousand seat grandstand constructed. Advertised as 'Buffalo Bill's Wild West Show and Congress of Rough Riders of the World', it contained re-enactments of attacks on wagon trains and stagecoach robberies, races and shooting displays – all whilst dressed in distinctive and colourful costumes. Female sharpshooter Annie Oakley, a headline act in her own right, also took part.

The *Liverpool Mercury* described the show as: 'A piece of the Wild West bodily transported to our midst. It is not a show in the ordinary acceptance of the term, because the actors are each and all real characters – men who have figured not on the stage, but in real life.'

Buffalo Bill came back to Liverpool in 1903, performing for three weeks at an exhibition site off Edge Lane.

JULY 7TH

1911: Aviator Henry Melly made the first non-stop flight from Liverpool to Manchester. The first person to attempt the flight had been American Samuel F. Cody in 1909, but after taking off from Aintree fog forced him to land at Prescot. Along with a passenger, A. Duckinfield, Melly took off in his Bleriot monoplane from Waterloo Sands and made the journey in forty minutes, becoming the first plane to land at the Trafford Park Aerodrome. For good measure, Melly then flew back to his Waterloo base in a time of sixty-three minutes.

The following day's *Daily Post* report was very short and to the point, saying: 'Mr Henry G. Melly yesterday accomplished with great ease the pioneer feat of flying from Waterloo to Manchester and back on his monoplane. On both journeys he carried a pupil as a passenger.'

On the one hundredth anniversary of the 1911 flight, five aircraft from the Liverpool Flying School commemorated the flight, taking off from Liverpool John Lennon Airport and flying to Waterloo, Trafford and back.

JULY 8TH

1901: It was reported that crime was rising in Liverpool as a result of a recent spell of hot weather. The *Liverpool Daily Courier*'s analysis said:

Hot weather invariably yields a large crop of criminal cases of a serious and petty character. The brilliant sunshine of Saturday and Sunday seems to have made this class of individuals restless and irritable, with the result that Mr Stewart, the Stipendiary, had about eighty charges before him yesterday morning. Most of them were for conduct which might have led to a grave breach of the peace had the police not interfered and taken the offending parties into custody. One prisoner after another stepped into the dock with the same excuse for the offence – that of having been too excited under the trying circumstances or having been drunk, which is worse. Mr Stewart however deals seriously with these wrongdoers without exception. It is very rare indeed that any offender receives any mercy at his hands and the fines imposed are often so heavy as to be beyond the powers of the prisoners to pay and they must therefore go to gaol.

JULY 9TH

1971: Liverpool City Council confirmed that local museums and art galleries would continue to be free to enter despite government plans to introduce charges.

A white paper had announced plans to charge 20p admission to all national collections, but with the Liverpool Museum and Walker Art Gallery coming under local authority control it was confirmed that they would not be affected. That evening's *Liverpool Echo* reported that Alderman Howard Hughes of the General Purposes Committee stated that although the council had the power to charge admission they chose not to, because: 'It is alright to charge admission in tourist places such as London, Edinburgh and York but if we were charging people here they would be paying double by the rates and through the door.'

Now Liverpool's museums do come under national control but remain free, despite the fact that the city now attracts millions of tourists annually (unlike in 1971).

JULY 10TH

1964: The Beatles made a triumphant return to Liverpool, appearing on the steps of the Town Hall where a civic reception was held for them before they attended the premiere of their film, *A Hard Day's Night*, at the Odeon cinema.

Since their last appearance in the city at the Liverpool Empire in December 1963, they had conquered the USA and also toured Australia. Crowds began to gather near the Town Hall some nine hours before the scheduled appearance, whilst others attended the airport, where the group arrived on a scheduled flight en route to Glasgow around 5 p.m. The following day's *Daily Post* headlined it 'THE NIGHT OF 100,000 SCREAMS', and said it was the city's craziest night since Everton won the FA Cup in 1933. It reported: 'The Beatles got a tumultuous reception and welcome home from the people of Liverpool last night after an absence of seven months. Mr Joseph Smith the city's Chief Constable said it was by far the biggest thing he could remember.'

The Beatles were unable to remain back in Liverpool very long however: just two nights later they had a concert to perform in Brighton.

JULY 11TH

1913: King George V visited Liverpool, opening the first phase of Gladstone Dock.

The dock, by the mouth of the river, was built to bring the port into the twentieth century and was capable of hosting the largest passenger liners. The first section completed was the graving dock, where ships are repaired. The dock was named after Robert Gladstone, chairman of the Dock Board. After visiting the Botanic Gardens, St George's Hall and the Town Hall, at 2.30 p.m. he boarded the *Galatea*, which sailed past the berthed *Mauretania* and up the River Mersey. Crowds lined both sides of the river whilst aviator Henry G. Melly flew overhead in his plane. When the *Galatea* reached the dock the King and Queen stood on the captain's bridge as it broke the ribbon to enter. The following day's *Liverpool Daily Courier* reported the King's thoughts on the day: Liverpool was the greatest port in the world and had 'docks which bear witness to the energy and efficiency of Liverpool people'.

Due to the First World War, Gladstone Dock was not fully completed until 1927. Robert Gladstone never saw its completion, dying almost six years to the day after George V's visit, on 12 July 1919.

JULY 12TH

1819: Violence broke out in Liverpool as the Orange Parade was attacked by stone-throwing Irish Catholics.

This was the first parade to commemorate the Battle of the Boyne by the Orange Order in Liverpool, although parades had occurred before in Bolton and Manchester. *Billinge's Liverpool Advertiser* reported on 19 July:

> After divine service, the procession formed again in Church Street and accompanied by a concourse of people marched up Lord Street, through Castle Street, round the Town Hall and down Dale Street. The crowd at the bottom of the latter street was very great, among which were observed a great number of the lower order of Irishmen. In a moment the procession was assailed by a shower of bricks and other missiles. The leader of the mob then, followed by a numerous band, rushed among the members of the society, knocked down and then trampled on any who opposed them. Happily no lives fell sacrifice to the fury of the mob. Many of the Orangemen were however seriously wounded.

Disturbances between Protestants and Catholics were a feature of many parades during the 1800s but today they pass off far more peacefully.

JULY 13TH

1945: Children playing on bomb-damaged ground in Great Homer Street made startling discovery when they found the skeleton of a man inside an iron tube. Under the headline 'DEAD MAN IN CYLINER MYSTERY BAFFLES POLICE', the following day's *Daily Post* explained:

> The discovery was made as a result of the curiosity of one of three small boys who had been rolling the cylinder about, causing him to try and find out what it contained. The first thing he saw was a boot and a bone and in consequence of this, information was given to police. The cylinder and its gruesome contents were removed to the city mortuary for further investigation. Inside the police found laid out, as in a lying posture, human bones from which all the flesh had rotted away, but adhering to them were pieces of clothing. The advanced state of decomposition suggested that the man died many years ago.

Locals told the paper the cylinder had been there for a considerable time and used as a seat by people unaware of its gruesome contents.

Given the documentation found in the clothing, the skeleton would appear to have been that of Thomas Creen Williams of Anfield, whose Leeds Street firm of oil merchants, T.C. Williams and Co., was being probed by accountants in the 1880s. However, it remains a mystery as to how he came to be in the tube, in which he probably died from asphyxiation.

JULY 14TH

1897: A milk dealer was heavily fined after he appeared in court for selling adulterated milk. The *Liverpool Mercury* reported the following day:

Abram Chapman, milk dealer of Douro Place, was summoned for having sold adulterated milk. Inspector Baker visited the defendant's premises on 24th June last and purchased a pint of new milk, which on analysis was found to have had fifteen parts of water added to every hundred parts of the poorest milk. Mr H. Neale, who defended, stated that his client had foolishly purchased some milk from a man selling it from a can in the street and the pint that the inspector received was a portion of that milk. Mr Stewart inflicted a penalty of £5 and costs.

JULY 15TH

1903: Seven people were killed and over one hundred injured when a train derailed at Waterloo. The 4.30 p.m. Liverpool to Southport express was approaching Waterloo Station at about 50mph when it derailed. It went up the ramp of the platform and knocked down the supports of a footbridge over the track. Extensive damage was caused to the engine and front two carriages. Six passengers and the engine fireman were killed, whilst the driver was amongst the 112 injured. The *Liverpool Daily Courier* reported:

> One of the most disastrous railway accidents in Liverpool and district for many years occurred yesterday afternoon. Looking at the massive wreckage it was amazing that anyone in these two coaches escaped with their lives. Those who did come out alive regard their escape as quite miraculous. The groans of injured men and women, some of them in the last agonies of death, were heartening to listen to. First aid was rendered and the more serious cases removed to Bootle Hospital whilst others, once bandaged up and attended to, were sent on to Southport on a later train.

The official report into the accident concluded that a faulty wheel spring was the most likely cause of the derailment.

JULY 16TH

1930: The Liverpool Co-operative Society was fined for allowing eight of its female workers to work longer than their regulated hours. The *Daily Post and Mercury* reported the following day:

The Liverpool Co-operative Society were fined £8 by the Stipendiary yesterday for an infringement of the Factory Act by employing eight women after the specified hours. It was stated that an inspector found the women in the society's tailoring factory in Byrom Street, working at 5.12 p.m. on Saturday 31 May. They should have finished work at 4 p.m. They were finishing some work in the dining room. Mr Hervert J. Davis, for the society, said notices were posted stating that anybody breaking the regulations as to hours would be liable to dismissal. The women went into the dining room of their own accord and without the knowledge of the management, because they were anxious to finish the work.

JULY 17TH

1792: There was an unseasonal sudden violent hailstorm that broke windows and destroyed crops. *Williamson's Liverpool Advertiser* reported on 23 July:

> On Tuesday this town and neighbourhood were visited by a tremendous storm. About half after six the aspect of the heavens was mild and clear. Suddenly a cloud appeared in the western horizon, which swelling and blackening in its progress, in a few minutes involved the hemisphere in gloom and discharged a mingled tempest of rain and hail. The stones which fell were as singular in their form as their size: some very large and forked. A gust of wind drove the hailstones with impetuous fury against every opposing object and shattered the windows of several houses. Mr Clegg's house at Kirkdale, the Reverend Heathcote's at Walton, Mr Richmond's and Mr Fazakerley's at Fazakerley felt its full force. The produce of whole gardens and crops of corn have been nearly destroyed.

There was a further storm the next day, when lightning struck a barn in Warbreck Moor where people were sheltering, but thankfully nobody was injured.

JULY 18TH

1934: Liverpool's road links were improved considerably when both the Queensway Tunnel and East Lancashire Road were opened by King George V.

The East Lancashire Road linked Liverpool with Manchester and was the first dual carriageway in the country linking two cities. The tunnel had been under construction since 1925, linking Liverpool with Birkenhead, and it was the longest underwater tunnel in the world. The King's day began in Salford: he opened the East Lancashire Road before travelling down it towards Liverpool, where he stopped to perform an opening ceremony for Walton Hall Park.

However, it was the tunnel that was attracting all the interest and it was estimated that a quarter of a million people witnessed its inauguration. The following day's *Daily Post and Mercury* reported that the opening 'will feature for centuries in the proud records of Merseyside'. After opening the tunnel the King was taken through it to Birkenhead, where he opened the central library. After his departure from Merseyside the King declared that he could not recall a greater display of affectionate loyalty during his reign.

JULY 19TH

1911: The Royal Liver Building, Britain's first office skyscraper, opened. The building had taken three years to build and was the new headquarters of the Royal Liver Assurance Group. Some had felt the design of the building, which was to be made of re-enforced concrete, was unworkable, but it took just three years to complete. The following day's *Daily Post and Mercury*, referring to it as 'one wonderful building', reported:

> Lord Sheffield, who three years ago had laid the foundation stone of the Royal Liver Building at the Pier Head, yesterday formally opened the eleven storey block in the presence of a large and enthusiastic assemblage. Lord Sheffield was very cordially received. Having expressed his thanks for the very beautiful key, he congratulated the delegates. His lordship, having wished prosperity to the undertaking, unlocked the doors amidst loud cheering.

The building went on to inspire many of the great skyscrapers of New York and Chicago. In 2011 its centenary was celebrated with a spectacular laser show but sadly the Royal Liver Assurance Co. moved out of Liverpool after their merger with Royal London.

JULY 20TH

1785: Italian Vincent Lunardi flew a hydrogen balloon over Prince's Dock. The first balloon flight had taken place in France in November 1783, and in September 1784 Lunardi took off in front of a crowd of 200,000 in London for a 24-mile flight to Hertfordshire accompanied by a cat, a dog and a caged pigeon.

Lunardi's planned ascension in the morning was postponed due to rain and thunder but by the afternoon the weather cleared and he gave notice of his intentions to try again at 5 p.m. The following day's *Williamson's Advertiser* reported that there was 'loud and repeated bursts of applause' as the balloon took off from the fort, and he 'gracefully waved his hat and saluted the spectators'. He remained in the air for fifty-five minutes – prolonging the time by disposing of his hat, waistcoat and shirt to save weight – before landing in a field in Simonswood, Kirkby. The *Mercury* reported that his clothes were recovered and that he was 'happy in having fulfilled his engagement with the Ladies and Gentlemen of Liverpool'.

Lunardi made another flight from Liverpool on 9 August before moving on to Glasgow and Edinburgh.

July 21st

1886: A freak thunderstorm occurred in Liverpool, leading to the death of two men in a sewer. The following day's *Liverpool Mercury* described how:

> One of the severest thunderstorms experienced for many years passed over Liverpool yesterday and did considerable damage to property in the lower parts of the city by the blocking of sewers and flooding of cellars. The sky was overcast throughout the morning and shortly after noon there were repeated claps of thunder. A few minutes after two o'clock commenced a tremendous downpour of rain, accompanied by vivid flashes of lightning. So heavy was the shower that within a few minutes the gutters overflowed and the grids were unable to carry away the immense volume of water which rushed down the streets in torrents.

The two men who died were Matthew Booth and Isaac Lloyd, who were repairing a sewer near the corner of Sefton Street and Northumberland Street. The *Mercury* reported:

> So sudden and terrific was the downpour that in a few minutes the sewer became swollen. The workmen made a rush to the mouth: three were successful after a great effort in escaping up the shaft into the street. They were horrified to discover that their comrades had been unable to escape up the shaft and were carried away by the force of the water rushing up the sewer.

JULY 22ND

1951: A special service was held in Liverpool Cathedral to celebrate the opening of the Liverpool Festival, part of the nationwide Festival of Britain celebrations.

The Festival of Britain was a series of events around the country to boost feelings of recovery and progress after the Second World War. It also marked the centenary of the 1851 Great Exhibition that was held at Crystal Palace.

The Festival was opened in London on 3 May but the Liverpool Festival was to run from 22 July to 12 August. Events included firework displays, naval demonstrations, concerts, plays, circuses and a three-day show at Wavertree Park.

In the morning 6,000 people attended an opening service conducted by the Archbishop of York, while other events on the opening day included a brass band, a parade of elephants heading to a circus and the chance to go aboard six warships. The following day's *Daily Post* noted:

> It was appropriate that the spirit of the festival should begin in Liverpool's magnificent Anglican Cathedral with a special service of thanksgiving on the 27th anniversary of the consecration. The navy entertained more than 20,000 visitors in four hours in the afternoon. There were long queues to go on board the six warships.

JULY 23RD

1966: One of the greatest ever games in World Cup history took place at Goodison Park when Portugal came from 3-0 down to beat North Korea 5-3.

It was not the quarter final that the city was expecting to stage. Portugal had surprisingly won their group ahead of champions Brazil, whilst North Korea had stunned everybody by knocking out Italy. The Koreans took a shock first-minute lead, then hit two in quick succession midway through the half to go three up. However, Eusebio quickly pulled one back; he then scored a forty-third-minute penalty to leave the game finely balanced at the break. Within fifteen minutes of the restart Eusebio had scored two more – one of them a penalty – to put Portugal ahead – and with ten minutes remaining Jose Augusto scored a fifth. That evening's *Liverpool Echo* reported: 'The Koreans went off to a wonderful reception having done far better than anyone could have expected. It was as great a one man performance that has been seen on this ground for many years.' Forty-four years, later the two sides met again in the World Cup in South Africa, Portugal running out 7-0 winners.

July 24th

1845: A lawyer arriving in Liverpool from Wexford was arrested for bringing too much whisky through the port. The following day's court appearance was reported in the *Liverpool Daily Courier* on 30 July, under the headline of 'GENTLEMAN SMUGGLER':

Mr Richard Waddy Swan, a barrister, who had the previous evening arrived in Liverpool via the Wexford boat, was fined £25, a reduced penalty, under the Act For Removing Spirits Without a Permit, for having in his possession two gallons of proof whisky. The detection had been made by Mr Woodruffe, the active Import Surveyor. The gentleman said that he was quite unaware of his having such a quantity of spirits with him and did not know that he was liable to any penalty beyond forfeiture.

JULY 25TH

1785: The first mail coach left Liverpool for London from the Golden Lion Inn in Dale Street.

The coach departed at 4 a.m. and promised a journey time of thirty hours. It carried just four passengers, the coachmen and an armed guard. As a mail coach, it had right of way over anything else on the road and was exempt from tolls. The announcement in *Gore's Liverpool Advertiser* on 21 July stated:

> All carters, coach boys etc. between Liverpool and London are to observe that when they hear the horn of the guard to the MAIL-COACH they are immediately to turn out of the road and make way. If this custom is not acceded to by the above mentioned they will be pursued as the law in that case directs.

JULY 26TH

1845: The SS *Great Britain*, the largest ship seen afloat to date, set sail from Liverpool for New York.

The ship had been designed by Isambard Kingdom Brunel. It was built of iron but had a screw propeller – ocean-going ships usually only boasted one or the other. Although she was launched in 1843, there were delays in fitting her out (in part caused by the ship being simply too big to fit into the docks where she needed to go). When she eventually set sail from Liverpool, there were only forty-five passengers aboard out of a capacity of three hundred and sixty. The *Liverpool Daily Courier* reported on 30 July: 'The ship moved slowly down the river, amidst the cheering of the spectators. Rounding the Rock Lighthouse, while entering the Rock Channel, the brilliance of the scene surpassed description.'

The following year she ran aground and the losses incurred as a result forced the Great Western Steamship Co. to sell her. By the end of the century she was not seaworthy and being used as a coal bunker in the Falkland Islands, but she was salvaged in 1970 and returned to Bristol where she is now a museum.

JULY 27TH

1990: Commuters faced an unusual reason for not going to work, as they found themselves locked in a station!

That evening's *Liverpool Echo* reported that travellers arriving at Bank Hall Station found the gates locked and the walls too high to climb over – with others outside waiting to get in. The situation was eventually resolved at 7.40 a.m. when a train driver was able to alert somebody. One lady, a nursery manager, was given a lift to work in a Merseyrail van. She commented: 'This really takes some beating. For once everything was running smoothly, then we couldn't get out of the station.' Merseyrail's explanation of the situation was 'that a leading railman had not left the keys the night before'.

July 28th

1962: There was travel chaos on the first day of the school summer holidays as the big getaway began and people queued all night for ferries. The *Liverpool Echo* reported that evening:

> There was a big holiday exodus from Liverpool today, the first weekend of the school holidays coinciding with a break in work for many trades. There were all night queues at the Prince's landing stage for the Isle of Man steamers and bus and railway stations and Liverpool Airport were also busy.

Traffic on the roads flowed relatively smoothly – unlike in the South West, where tailbacks of 20 miles built up – but it was a different story for public transport locally. Stalls selling tea and coffee did a roaring trade as people waited for Isle of Man ferries, four of which were due to sail in the morning. Queues stretched from the landing stage to the Liver Buildings and didn't ease until lunchtime.

The *Echo* reported an Isle of Man Steam Packet spokesman as saying 'it had been the busiest morning for five years', and that the airport, railway stations and bus depots were busy too, with a Lime Street official commenting, 'I think there is more holiday traffic than this time last year'. Exchange station was thronged too, with people making an early start for the Scottish resorts.

JULY 29TH

1848: The class system was exposed at Lime Street Station when a man was refused permission to see his family members onto a train. The man, calling himself 'A LOVER OF JUSTICE' had the following letter published in the *Liverpool Mercury* on 8 August:

> On Sunday morning last I went to the Lime Street railway station to see part of my family off to London by the half past nine train. After paying the fares I presented myself with them at the entrance from the office to the yard where a police man blocked up the way and refused to allow me to pass to see them off by the train simply because they were third class passengers. The friends of the first class passengers were freely admitted, and obsequiously attended to. Why this offensive distinction should be made I know not, neither do I know whether the directors have any legal authority to prevent persons from entering the yard with their friends who are going off. Thousands are aggrieved by the shameful and tyrannous conduct of the company.

JULY 30TH

1846: The Albert Dock was opened by Queen Victoria's husband Prince Albert in what was the first state royal visit to Liverpool.

The dock was revolutionary in that it was surrounded by warehouses into which goods could be directly loaded from ships. The warehouses were built entirely of cast iron, brick and stone with no wood, making them virtually fireproof. Of the scene before the opening, the *Liverpool Daily Courier* explained on 31 July: 'From almost every window of the immense piles of warehouse flags were displayed. Nothing could exceed it in grandeur or effect, it was a gorgeous spectacle.'

Prince Albert entered on the royal yacht *Fairy*, described as a truly imposing site and said to those gathered: 'The recollection of the splendid sight I have witnessed today will never be effaced from my memory.' Times changed fast, however, and within fifty years the dock wasn't suitable for shipping any more, but the warehouses still provided valuable storage space. In 1972 they were closed for good but since the 1980s have been re-vamped into a major tourist attraction.

JULY 31ST

1919: A strike began amongst constables in Liverpool's police force. The background to the strike lay in terms and conditions. Police officers were earning the same as general labourers and less than dock workers, yet were directed to live in areas of the city where rents were higher, further reducing the standard of living.

The strike began late on the 31st – with 'dramatic suddenness', according to the *Liverpool Daily Courier* on 2 August – gaining further momentum on the 1st when emergency sessions were convened at the Town Hall involving the Lord Mayor, Watch Committee and Chief Constable. The *Courier* reported:

> It was learned late last night at Dale Street that the total number of strikers had reached 632 out of a total strength of 1,958. The Lord Mayor appeals to the citizens of Liverpool to assist him in the maintenance of law and order in the city. Volunteers for duty are asked to enrol from ten o'clock this morning.

All those officers who joined the action were sacked and it led to the Police Act later that year, making it illegal for police officers to join a trade union or go on strike.

AUGUST 1ST

1859: The training ship HMS *Conway* opened. Moored off Rock Ferry by the Mercantile Marine Service Associations (MMSA), the aim of the ship was to train boys for a career in the merchant navy. HMS *Conway*, a small warship, was lent to the MMSA for the purpose. The *Liverpool Mercury* revealed the next day: 'Yesterday this floating marine mercantile boarding school was formally inaugurated. A special steamer conveyed several members of the Mercantile Marine Association to the *Conway*. There was also on board the first instalment of scholars, some of whom had donned their uniform of blue with gilt anchor buttons.'

Chairman of the MMSA Captain Sproule told guests that he hoped in two years the ship would produce a set of boys that would not disgrace any ship in the kingdom. He also praised local merchants who agreed any *Conway* cadet taken would be considered to have had one year of service. After the formalities were concluded, the National Anthem was played as the special guests got back on board the steamer.

Just two years later this particular ship was replaced by HMS *Winchester*, but that took the *Conway* name – as did two further replacements in 1875 and 1953. From the Second World War, the HMS *Conway* was based at Anglesey.

AUGUST 2ND

1972: Liverpool city councillors voted against a motion to close the city's airport.

The Liberal Party were seeking the move, claiming that the airport had lost up to £4 million in the previous six years and that the land would be better being redeveloped so that it could generate income through the rates. Party leader Cyril Carr told councillors that the city would still have reasonable access to an airport.

However, the *Liverpool Echo* reported the following day that other parties were against the move, with Labour leader Alderman William Sefton said to have asked: 'If the Liberals were seriously trying to destroy an asset which would be vital to the city in a few years. Those trying to close and redevelop the airport should remember the many empty areas of the city already waiting developers.'

Alderman Stephen Minion of the Conservatives pointed out that the airport had recently seen a 10 per cent rise in passenger numbers and the motion was overwhelmingly defeated by ninety-six votes to thirteen.

Today Liverpool Airport is one of the top ten in the country, handling in excess of five million passengers a year.

AUGUST 3RD

1954: Liverpool Corporation workers began the annual task of clearing up a mountain of Bank Holiday litter.

The following day's *Daily Post* reported that 400 men were assigned to the task, with the level of the problem differing in various parts of the city. By the Pier Head, it was described as 'having paper, ice-cream cartons, bus tickets and bottles strewn everywhere'. However, this was lighter than the year before due to inclement weather and an intensive anti-litter drive in preceding months, in conjunction with the 'Keep Britain Tidy' campaign. It was a different story in the parks, where thousands had been after the sun came out later in the day. In Stanley Park, a spokesman from the Parks' Department claimed it had never been as bad: 'Litter is everywhere, on the playing fields around the lakes, in the gardens.'

Calderstones, Newsham and Sefton Parks were reported to be tidier than in recent years, but in Southport it was estimated that it would take a week to clear everything up.

AUGUST 4TH

1917: Captain Noel Chavasse died, two days after he was wounded when a shell entered an aid post where he was tending to others. Chavasse had already been awarded a Victoria Cross for his actions in 1916: he saved the lives of twenty wounded men whilst under heavy enemy fire.

In the early hours of 2 August Chavasse was at an aid post, where he had been rescuing wounded soldiers. After suffering major abdominal injuries he managed to crawl to another post for assistance but died at a casualty clearing station on the afternoon of 4 August. News of his death was made public in the *Liverpool Daily Courier* on 11 August, which reported: 'A feeling of profound regret will be occasioned throughout Liverpool with the news that Captain Noel Godfrey Chavasse VC, a son of the Bishop of Liverpool, has been killed in France. Captain Chavasse died a true soldiers' death, he fully lived up to that standard of British pluck and bravery.'

Chavasse's actions in the days immediately before his death led to him being posthumously awarded a second Victoria Cross, and his memory in Liverpool lives on, Chavasse Park being named after him.

AUGUST 5TH

1929: The Welsh Royal National Eisteddfod opened at Sefton Park. This was the third time, the others being 1884 and 1900, that the event had been held in the city, whose Welsh population was estimated at 75,000.

The *Daily Post* reported the next day that a record 7,800 attended on the first day, which included brass-band contests and singing events. There was some local success when the Edge Hill LMS Band finished second in their event. There was some humour in the opening speech by the Lord Mayor, Alderman Miller, who said:

> I am totally unacquainted with the Welsh language and nothing would please me more than to address you in your own ancient tongue but I see that in the programme the words '*Anglwydd Faer Lerpwl*' (Lord Mayor of Liverpool) are preceded by the words '*Y Bore*'. That is a new designation for me, although a lot of Lord Mayors have been and will be subject to adverse criticism.

Translated, 'y bore' means 'the morning'. Liverpool, or anywhere else in England, hasn't held an Eisteddfod since, proposals put forward to host it in 2007 being given only a lukewarm response at best.

AUGUST 6TH

1957: There was traffic chaos as a lorry overturned, spilling its load of empty beer bottles into the road. The *Daily Post* reported on the crash the following day:

An articulated lorry, carrying 1,200 crates of empty beer bottles, overturned at the junction of Allerton Road and Queens Drive last night. Fortunately there was nobody near as the vehicle broke away and capsized, sending scores of crates, each carrying 24 bottles, hurtling towards the road. Broken bottles littered the road. The lorry was returning to St Helens after collecting the crates in the city. The driver said he felt a sudden jolt and heard a big crash. Then he saw the articulated portion of the lorry lying on its side. Breakdown men were sent to clear the blockage and during this operation police diverted traffic.

AUGUST 7TH

1950: Over 8,000 people attended the Liverpool Co-operative Society's annual gala. It was held at Higher Lane in Fazakerley and believed to the one of the most successful organised by the society. The following day's *Daily Post* reported:

> Eight Liverpool footballers gave an exhibition of tennis heading and there was a display of gymnastics by the Liverpool Fire Service. Councillor J. Cresswell opened a flower show. The challenge cup, presented to a co-operative society employee gaining the highest number of points gained in sports events, was won by Mr G. A. Barton.

AUGUST 8TH

1867: There was a strange case in the County Court when a man tried to sue Brigham Young, head of the Church of the Latter Day Saints, more commonly known as the Mormons.

The case was brought about by a William Hall who lived in St Anne Street and claimed he was owed £1 12s in wages from the *Millennial Star* newspaper, which was distributed from the local Mormon quarters in Islington.

However, with Young in Salt Lake City there was a problem with the service of the summons. The following day's *Liverpool Mercury* reported that when the case was called:

> A gentleman appeared, who the Plaintiff called the 'Mormon Bishop of the district' and who he said had the entire management of the transactions of the Mormons and their business carried out on the address given. The gentleman said that Mr Young lived in America and declined to have his name substituted for that of Mr Young.

The court registrar suggested that the only way to resolve the matter was if 'the Plaintiff followed Mr Brigham Young to Salt Lake City or waited for him to come to this country'. With the summons unserved, the case was dismissed and it was left to Mr Hall to decide if he wished to use his resources to continue to pursue Mr Young.

AUGUST 9TH

1932: The *Evening Express* reported that ex-Liverpool servicemen were eager to sign up for the Bolivian and Paraguayan armies as the two countries fought a war.

The dispute, which became known as the Chaco War, had begun in June over the River Paraguay, needed by both landlocked countries to access the Pacific Ocean. Ex-army officers were wanted to train both countries' armies, with attractive offers of £4 10s a week (more than the average wage), bonuses and a first-class passage out. A Paraguayan Consulate official told the *Evening Express*: 'Two Liverpool men have visited the Paraguayan Consulate to enquire as to how they could join up. The Consul is away and we have no instructions here, [so] we are referring all inquirers to the Consul General in London.'

Far more interest was being shown at the Bolivian Consulate, who were offering a £50 joining bonus as opposed to Paraguay's £30. An official there said: 'We have two or three letters from Liverpool ex-flying officers and three or four others have called here. We have no instructions and can do nothing at the moment, [as] the Consul is in London today.'

The war went on for three years, Paraguay eventually gaining control of the disputed region.

AUGUST 10TH

1876: All Hallows' church in Allerton was consecrated. The church was paid for by shipping magnate John Bibby, who lived in nearby Harthill House, and designed by G.E. Grayson. The organ, encased in carved but unpolished oak, was built by Messrs Whitley of Chester. The following day's *Liverpool Mercury* reported of the consecration service:

> The new church of All Hallows, Allerton, built and endowed by Mr John Bibby, was consecrated yesterday by the Lord Bishop of Chester, in the morning when divine service was held. The architect has not only created a magnificent structure in every architectural detail but has succeeded in a point in which so many have failed – he has hit the happy medium of sound and for its acoustic properties, as proved yesterday, Allerton church certainly stands unsurpassed in this district. The bishop was received by the vicar, the patron and a member of the local clergy. His Lordship announced that he was ready to proceed to consecration, then walked down the central aisle and up the north aisle, reciting the 24th psalm.

The Bibby family are still connected to the church. The current patron is Michael Bibby, managing director of the Bibby Line Group and direct descendant of John Bibby's father.

AUGUST 11TH

1873: There was tragedy on board a steamer on hire to Cunard's Mediterranean line when the captain fell off the bridge to his death not long after leaving Liverpool. The death was reported as follows in the next day's *Liverpool Mercury*:

Captain Launcelot F. Pritchard, for many years a Captain in the Cunard service, was killed yesterday on board the steamer *Andres*, of which he was the Commander. The steamer was chartered by Messrs Burns and MacIver and left Liverpool yesterday on the evening tide, bound for Genoa. She reached the Bell Buoy about half past four o' clock, and while Captain Pritchard was standing on the bridge he accidentally fell from it to the deck, dislocating his neck by the fall, death ensuing almost instantaneously. After the melancholy occurrence the steamer put back and the body of the deceased gentleman was conveyed on shore.

AUGUST 12TH

1963: Thousands flocked to Liverpool Town Hall on one of the rare occasions its doors were thrown open to the public. The *Liverpool Echo* reported that night that plenty of schoolchildren were in attendance and that 20,000 visitors were expected over the week. However, no chances were being taken with the city's jewels, with plain-clothes detectives mingling with the public. The *Echo* stated that the 'priceless civic insignia' – consisting of a three maces, sword of state, silver oar and staves – were on show in the ballroom behind a roped-off table.

The council chamber seemed to be getting the most attraction, as well as a portrait of Queen Elizabeth II at the head of the main staircase. The Town Hall is now open far more often, with pre-booked tours being available on a monthly basis.

AUGUST 13TH

1911: The Riot Act was read on the steps of St George's Hall after disturbances broke out amongst a crowd attending a rally. The Transport Strike had been going on since June, involving dockers, railway workers and sailors (amongst others). The authorities had given permission for the rally, at which activist Tom Mann gave a speech.

The crowd had been peaceful, but disturbances began when a man was forcibly brought down from a window sill of the North Western Hotel. Officers and soldiers who had been drafted in from other cities had been concealed in the hall and baton-charged the crowd, leading to several injuries. The following day's *Liverpool Echo* described it as 'a scene which reminded one of the turbulent times in Paris when the Revolution was at its height'.

Stipendiary Magistrate Stuart Deacon then addressed the crowd and read out the Riot Act, ordering everybody to disperse otherwise the authorities would take whatever steps necessary to ensure they did. Two days later two men were shot dead by troops in Vauxhall following a disturbance when a prison van carrying some of those arrested was attacked. The strike finally came to an end on 24 August.

AUGUST 14TH

1891: Thousands of employees of the Bass brewery in Burton on Trent visited Liverpool as the city was chosen as the destination of the company's annual excursion. Thirteen special trains arrived between 8 a.m. and 10 a.m., but there was disappointment for many who arrived to find it raining, the weather having been clear and dry in Burton. The *Liverpool Mercury* reported the following day:

Between six and seven thousand work people, their wives, children and friends visited Liverpool. Elaborate arrangements had been made for the comfort of the party. The chiefs of the different parts of the brewery had charge of the several companies into which the party was divided. Descriptive programmes had been printed, which contained ample information for the benefit of those who wished to employ their time in seeing the sights of Liverpool. Despite the downpour of rain the excursionists made the best of their time. The river was, of course, the chief centre of attraction. Eastham proved to be a special attraction on the part of the great desire of visitors to see the Manchester Ship Canal. Each employee was presented with an illustrated guide to the canal. In the evening the excursionists returned to Burton by trains leaving Central Station every quarter of an hour.

August 15th

1836: Lime Street Station opened, leading to the closure of Crown Street after just six years. The overwhelming success of the Liverpool & Manchester Railway had meant that Crown Street was no longer adequate, being too small and far from the city centre. Lime Street Station was developed on land purchased from Liverpool Corporation by the Liverpool & Manchester Railway for £9,000. Construction of the tunnel from Edge Hill began in 1832.

The opening of the terminus was given surprisingly little coverage by the *Liverpool Mercury*, the full extent of whose report on 19 August was:

> The new station in Lime Street, for the arrival and departure of the railway trains, was opened on Monday last. The time occupied in passing through the tunnel, which is about one mile and a quarter in length, is from five to seven minutes. There is not the slightest inconvenience felt in proceeding through it. Lights are attached to the sides of the carriages. Crowds of persons assembled at Edge Hill to witness the arrival of the trains.

Lime Street remains in use today as the city's rail gateway for long distance passengers. Although Crown Street never opened again to passengers, it was used as a coal depot until 1972.

AUGUST 16TH

1975: There was a boost for the Ford car factory in Halewood when it was announced that export sales for the Ford Escort were booming. The Escort was the third Ford model that had been built at Halewood since its opening in 1963, following on from the Anglia and Corsair. The *Liverpool Echo* reported that evening:

> A spate of orders received at Ford's export offices in Warley, Essex, have brought total overseas orders to £35 million. The figure includes £10 million worth of Escorts which will be shipped to Europe from Halewood. Mr Maurice Sury, manager of overseas markets planning, said, 'We have just been informed of orders worth nearly £20 million from Far East customers alone. Malaysia, Taiwan and the Philippines already require over 7,000 Escorts between them. Australia has asked for 9,500. New Zealand wants 6,800.'

Although Fords are no longer produced at Halewood, the plant still produces cars for Land Rover and Jaguar, now part of the India-based Tata Group.

AUGUST 17TH

1853: A policeman appeared in court charged with smuggling. The *Liverpool Mercury* reported on 19 August:

> Police Officer James Lynch, James Jordan and Elizabeth McHugh were fined 10s and costs for smuggling whisky. The prisoner Jordan went on board the *Dundalk* steamer, lying in the Clarence Dock, on Tuesday evening and procured a bottle of whisky which he transferred to the police officer, who gave it to the female prisoner. She was stopped while taking it on shore.

AUGUST 18TH

1927: An inquest took place into a tragic suicide in which a man killed himself after being unable to find work due to his age. That evening's *Evening Express* reported:

A verdict of suicide was recorded today at the inquest today concerning the death from gas poisoning of Thomas Ewens, aged 68, a former Corporation plate-later living in Alderville Road. Ewens it was stated went to Australia two years ago to visit his daughter. He returned in April and had since been unable to obtain work. A few days ago he said, 'I think I am getting too old to get work'. He was found dead yesterday by his niece, with whom he lived. He was lying in the back kitchen with a flexible gas tube in his mouth. The City Coroner said there was not sufficient evidence to show the man's state of mind.

AUGUST 19TH

1951: Widow Beatrice Rimmer was brutally murdered at her home in Cranborne Road, Wavertree.

Beatrice had been seen about 7 p.m. returning to her home after visiting her son in Dingle. The next day, when her milk was still sitting on her doorstep, neighbours became worried, and her son later found her lying in a pool of blood. The *Daily Post* reported on 21 August:

> Mrs Beatrice Alice Rimmer, aged 54, of 7 Cranborne Road Wavertree, was found dead in the passage of her home last night. She had died from severe head injuries. Every available policeman and detective was on duty early today making a thorough search of every street, back entry and blitz site in the neighbourhood of the house. They were seeking the weapon by which Mrs Rimmer had been battered to death.

Two Mancunians, Edward Devlin and Alfred Burns, were later hanged for the murder. However, doubts have been raised over the safety of the convictions and they have been the subject of a book, *Murderers or Martyrs*, by George Skelly, published in October 2011.

AUGUST 20TH

1891: John Conway was hanged at Walton Gaol for the murder of nine-year-old Nicholas Martin.

Conway, a sixty-two-year-old marine fireman, had butchered Nicholas and put his body and the murder weapons in a kitbag before throwing it into the docks. Conway pleaded guilty to murder and was sentenced to death. The hanging was a botched affair that almost saw Conway's head torn off. The following day's *Liverpool Mercury* reported that Conway said 'beware of drink' as the executioner placed a hood over his head, but was denied the opportunity to say any more. After the lever was pulled, the *Mercury* shocked its readers by sharing the following story: 'Reporters observed that the head of the condemned man was nearly severed from the body. Beneath there was a great accumulation of blood.'

The hangman James Berry left the prison without waiting for the inquest to begin and refused to answer reporters' questions later. He resigned his position as hangman about a month afterwards.

AUGUST 21ST

1921: Miss Adelaide Watt of Speke Hall died. Miss Watt had lived there since she came of age in 1878 and took a keen interest in the estate and the welfare of her tenants, most of whom were involved in farming. Speke Hall had been bought by her great-great-uncle Richard Watt, who owned a sugar plantation in the West Indies. Her death notice in the following day's *Evening Express* was very simple, reading: 'August 21st at Speke Hall, aged 64 years, Adelaide Watt of Speke Hall Lancashire and of Spott House Haddingtonshire. Only child of the late Richard Watt of Speke Hall and of Bishop Burton, Yorkshire. Internment at Speke church (date later).'

With Watt never having married, it was bequeathed in her will to descendants of the Norris family, the hall's original owners, who were allowed to enjoy it for twenty-one years before it was to pass to the National Trust, who still own the building today.

AUGUST 22ND

1964: As The Beatles took America by storm, there were rumours that their manager Brian Epstein was looking to take over another local band, The Searchers. That evening's *Liverpool Echo* reported how Epstein had told them from Seattle: 'Certain negotiations have taken place and I expect to have them completed by the time I go back on 30th August.' However, the news was a mystery to The Searchers themselves, who had had three number ones to date. They told the paper: 'We've heard nothing about it. We might find out something later but at the moment we just don't know a thing.'

The takeover didn't happen, and although The Searchers got to number three in the charts later in the year with 'When You Walk in the Room' they were never as successful again.

AUGUST 23RD

1938: A female loan shark who, it was said, instilled fear into her clients was heavily fined.

The court heard that forty-seven-year-old Annie Williams of Westminster Road had charged 5s a week interest, equating to 650 per cent per annum, on a loan of £2. The prosecutor alleged that three other women had borrowed small sums but were too frightened of Williams to give evidence against her. That day's *Evening Express* reported how Williams pleaded guilty to being 'a moneylender without a licence', but her solicitor had told the court that:

> The women pestered her to lend them money to get them out of the hands of landlords and to redeem their husbands' clothes from pawn. She herself borrowed the money to give it to them. She denied having charged the interest alleged. She received only a few odd shillings for drink.

Williams was fined £25 and given three months to pay.

AUGUST 24TH

1914: A new battalion of soldiers marched through Liverpool as the recruitment drive went on.

War had been declared on Germany three weeks earlier, leading to many local men seeking to enlist for service. Those that did formed the 11th Service Battalion of the King's Liverpool Regiment. The following day's *Liverpool Daily Courier* reported: 'A considerable impetus was given to the recruiting in Liverpool yesterday by the procession of newly recruited men, who marched from the recruiting office in St James Place, by way of Old Haymarket to Scotland Road centre.' The men were described as 'promising young fellows who had about them the bearing of really fine soldiers'. The *Courier* felt that Liverpool should rightly be proud of itself, commenting: 'Considering the number of men who are already serving their country, it is most praiseworthy to think Liverpool has been able to raise another battalion in little over a week.'

Recruitment did gather further pace, spearheaded by Lord Derby, as seven more service battalions were formed by the end of the year.

AUGUST 25TH

1865: There was a mutiny amongst the crew of a ship bound for New York – one which broke out before it had even left the River Mersey. The *Liverpool Mercury* shared the story on the following day:

> It seems that some of the sailors were in drink and when the Second Mate ordered them to go to work they refused, when a row ensued. It is said that the Second Mate knocked three of the seamen down and injured them severely. One of the crew was taken to the Northern Hospital having received severe injuries during the melee. The Second Mate was overpowered by the crew and was very roughly handled, his jaw being broken and other injuries inflicted upon him. When it became known that a disturbance had taken place on board the vessel the river police at once put off but by the time they had reached the vessel order had been restored.

AUGUST 26TH

1979: Crowds flocked to Liverpool Airport for a glimpse of the supersonic jet Concorde.

The Air France Concorde had been specially chartered by a local travel agency for package deals and the visit coincided with the 60th anniversary of commercial flights between Britain and France. It was the first time a Concorde aircraft had been to Liverpool and the first Air France Concorde to visit a regional airport.

The *Daily Post* reported the following day that the flight from Paris to Liverpool had taken just under an hour with the sound barrier being broken for a short time. Of the crowds who turned out to welcome her, it said:

> Thousands along the river saw it arrive and take off again, the huge crowds causing traffic hold ups. Some motorists queued for more than an hour to get out of the airport car park. On Eastham Ferry there were several thousand thronging the roads and fields overlooking the Manchester Ship Canal and right opposite the airport.

Concorde soon became an annual visitor to Liverpool for the Grand National before being withdrawn from service after the crash of one of its planes.

AUGUST 27TH

1910: Thousands attended Liverpool landing stage to witness the return of fugitive Dr Crippen and his lover Ethel le Neve, wanted in connection of the murder of his wife.

Crippen had fled to Canada on the discovery of a corpse under the cellar of his London home. However, police officers took a faster boat and were able to arrest him on deck at Montreal. The case made history as it was the first time a wireless radio message was used to snare a suspect, with the captain of the ship on which he was on board sending a message back regarding his suspicions. Crippen arrived in Liverpool on board the *Megantic* on a Saturday afternoon, with the *Daily Post and Mercury* reporting on 29 August: 'The arrival of Crippen and Miss Le Neve was fraught with a widespread interest probably unprecedented in the history of the port.'

However, very few managed to get a glimpse of the couple as they were quickly taken down the luggage ramp, whilst all eyes were focused on the passenger gangway. Crippen was sentenced to death, while Le Neve was cleared of being an accessory after the fact.

AUGUST 28TH

1207: Liverpool came into being when King John granted a Charter giving it privileges such as the right to hold fairs and markets. The Charter was just seven inches long and three inches wide and written in Latin. A translation reads:

John, by the grace of God, King of England, Lord of Ireland, Duke of Normandy, Aquitan, and Earl of Anjou, to all our faithful subjects who may have been willing to hold burgage houses at the town of Liverpool, greeting. Know ye, that we have granted to all our faithful subjects who have taken burgage houses at Liverpool that they may have all the liberties and free customs in the town of Liverpool, which any other free borough upon the sea has, in our territories. And therefore we command you, that securely and in our peace, you may come tither, to receive and dwell in our burgage houses; in witness thereof, we transmit to you these our letters-patent. Witness – Simon de Pateshill: at Winchester, the twenty eighth day of August, in the ninth year of our reign.

AUGUST 29TH

1849: A woman was sentenced to one month's imprisonment for taking seamens' clothes off a vessel and pawning them. The *Liverpool Mercury* reported on 31 August that Margaret Moore had gone aboard the *Shannon* and managed to obtain many uniforms – as well as £4 – on the pretence of having them cleaned, claiming that she had been employed by many American captains.

However, instead she pawned the clothes for 20s before being apprehended in Warrington. The *Mercury* reported of the sentence being carried out: 'The female prisoner was sentenced to one months' imprisonment and the pawnbroker was reprimanded for taking the clothes in. The seamen had their clothes restored to them without any reward to the pawnbroker who was liable to a penalty.'

AUGUST 30TH

1977: The Copperas Hill mail-sorting office opened. The £1 million purpose-built building meant that mail sorting would now be done electronically (as opposed to by hand as at the previous base in Victoria Street). That evening's *Liverpool Echo* reported:

> Liverpool's mail went electronic today when the Post Office's new sorting depot opened in Copperas Hill. When Copperas Hill becomes fully operational in the autumn thousands of letters will be electronically sorted by coding machines and divided into appropriate pigeon holes. Copperas Hill we be one of just six sites selected in Britain's cities for a massive switch from hand to machine sorting as part of a Post Office mechanisation drive over the next twelve months. Mechanisation is not expected to speed up delivery but will cut the cost as much of the sorting is at present done in the evening at high rates.

The Copperas Hill sorting office closed in 2010 with workers transferred to Warrington. The building has now been sold to John Moores University.

AUGUST 31ST

1715: Liverpool's first dock opened. Designed by Thomas Steers, it was the first commercial wet dock in the world, and 200 yards long and 90 yards wide at its widest point. Holding up to 100 ships, the dock was accessed by iron gates 23ft by 34ft that were opened at high tide.

It had come about by after merchants petitioned the House of Commons for a Bill in 1709. The House of Commons' Journal states that the wording of the petition said:

> A petition of the Mayor, Aldermen and merchants of, and trading to and from the port of Liverpool in the County Palatine of Lancaster was presented to the house and read, setting forth that they had sustained great losses for want of a good harbour, the same lying open to the violence of the west and north-west winds; to prevent which they conceive a convenient dock may be made there, wherein their ships may lie safe; and be that end the Corporation of Liverpool have granted a sufficient quantity of waste ground; and praying that leave may be given to bring in a Bill to enable the Corporation of Liverpool to place buoys and landmarks at or near the entrance into the said port, and to perfect a convenient dock for security of all ships trading tither.

Royal Assent was given on 24 March 1710, and Bryan Blundell's diary records that the *Mulberry* was the first ship to enter the dock. It was closed in 1826 to enable the building of a Customs House.

SEPTEMBER 1ST

1760: The first stagecoach service from Liverpool began connecting the town with Warrington and Manchester. The route had become a possibility thanks to improvements to the turnpike road between Prescot and Warrington and was run by John Stonehewer and James France. An advert in *Williamson's Advertiser* on 5 September announced the start of the route:

Manchester, Warrington, Prescot and Liverpool MACHINE sets out on Monday September 1st, 1760 and every Monday and Thursday morning at six o'clock from Mr Budworth's, the Bulls Head Inn, in Manchester; will call at the Red Lion Inn in Warrington; at Mr Reynolds's, the old Legs of Man in Prescot; and lies at Mr Banner's the Golden Fleece in Liverpool. Returns from there every Tuesday and Friday morning at six o'clock and calls at the above places on its way back to Manchester. Each passenger to pay 8*s*. To be allowed 14Ib weight of luggage and all above to pay 1*d* per pound.

SEPTEMBER 2ND

1996: The North Western Hotel in Lime Street re-opened as student accommodation after lying empty for sixty years. Built by the London & North Western Railway in 1871 and with 330 rooms, it closed in 1933. Eventually it was bought by John Moores University for £6 million in 1994 and converted into student accommodation.

The opening ceremony was performed by ninety-one year old Francis McKeown, who had been an apprentice chimney sweep at the hotel in 1922.

The *Liverpool Echo* reported of its new lease of life that evening:

> The former North Western Hotel opened for business today – the first time in sixty years. The first guests were arriving as it reopened as student digs. More than 240 students from John Moores University will live at the North Western Hall, next to Lime Street station. The £8 million refurbishment has taken eighteen months and involved painstaking restoration to return the building to its former glory.

The accommodation, comprising of three to five bedroomed flats, is now available to students of any of the city's universities.

SEPTEMBER 3RD

1874: The Jewish Synagogue on Princes Road was consecrated. There had been a Jewish community in Liverpool for over 100 years, but they had now outgrown their synagogue in Seel Street, which could seat only 290 people. The new building was able to accommodate 824 and was built on land purchased from the Earl of Sefton. The following day's *Liverpool Mercury* reported of the opening:

> A rarely seen and interesting ceremony of the Jewish religion was witnessed in Liverpool yesterday, when the new and beautiful synagogue was formally consecrated and opened for public worship. The synagogue may safely be pronounced one of the most beautiful and elaborate ecclesiastical structures in Liverpool. Shortly after one o' clock the Chief Rabbi of the United Kingdom, the Rev. Dr N. Adler and the ministers and office bearers of the church assembled in one of the rooms of the vestibule and were formed into a procession. The Chief Rabbi took the leading position. As it passed under a small canopy the reader chanted in solemn tones in the Hebrew tongue, passages from the psalms. At the close of the service the Chief Rabbi entered the pulpit and preached in English.

The synagogue continues to be a place of worship today.

SEPTEMBER 4TH

1934: The people of Liverpool were warned they still needed to save water despite some rainfall in recent days. That day's *Evening Express* reported that Colonel F. Hibbert, the city's water engineer, told the Water Committee:

> The public must still exercise the utmost economy in the use of water. The stock of water in the reservoirs has increased during the two months by 40,000,000 gallons and is 507,000,000 gallons less than it was on September 1st 1933. Whilst the position at Rivington is slightly better than it was on 1st July, it does not warrant the removal of the present restrictions and the public must still exercise the utmost economy in the use of water. There is a tendency in wet weather for customers to relax their efforts to save and this has been noticeable in the last week or two. Consumers must realise that our stocks are not as high as they were last year and it is still important that we save as much as we can.

Councillor B. V. Kirby, presiding over the meeting, responded by saying: 'We are actually worse off now than we were twelve months ago and the public must be strictly economical in their use of water.'

SEPTEMBER 5TH

1960: Television personality Bruce Forsyth announced that he would be giving 100 per cent commitment to Liverpool for his forthcoming run in a pantomime at the Liverpool Empire. In an interview with the *Liverpool Echo*, he said that he would not be continuing his stint as host of the popular television show *Sunday Night at the London Palladium*: 'If I travelled down to London each weekend it would mean getting the night sleeper on a Saturday night and returning on the Sunday night sleeper – and with a whole day of rehearsals before the actual performance on the Sunday evening.'

Before his stint in pantomime Forsyth first had to complete his summer season in Blackpool but confirmed he intended to have a long overdue months' holiday with his wife first. More than fifty years on, he is still entertaining the viewers and has been knighted for his services to entertainment.

September 6th

1877: The Walker Art Gallery opened. Named after its benefactor Sir Andrew Barclay Walker, the gallery was built to house the town council's art collection. There was a great deal of excitement about the opening, with the *Liverpool Mercury* reporting the following day:

> The scene in front of the art gallery was one of the most remarkable that has been witnessed in Liverpool for many years. Early in the forenoon the crowds began to assemble in Lime Street and the neighbourhood and from the numbers that quickly arrived it soon became evident that the precautions that had been taken by the erection of barricades were not unnecessary.

The crowds witnessed a display of marching and bands before the Earl of Derby declared the building open. This was followed by a performance of the 100th psalm by the Liverpool Vocalists Union then there was loud cheering from the crowd. In the evening there was a grand banquet at St George's Hall whilst 2,500 ticket holders, described by the *Mercury* as 'of the most respectable class of working men', were allowed into the gallery.

The gallery today houses one of the largest art collections in the country outside of London.

September 7th

1895: Wavertree Playground, commonly known as 'The Mystery' due to its benefactor remaining anonymous, was opened in front of a crowd of 20,000. The opening festivities of the 100+ acre site involved a huge garden party and fête, sports races and fireworks display. The *Liverpool Mercury* reported on 9 September:

> The opening of the Wavertree Playground, the gift of a generous citizen whose retiring disposition prevented the association of either his name or presence with a remarkable opening ceremony, took place on Saturday afternoon in glorious weather. The opening ceremony was on a scale worthy of what the Lord Mayor, in a well compressed speech, described as 'by far the most notable gift the city has ever received'. Visitors were impressed with the size and beauty of the playground.

Whilst performing the opening ceremony with a golden key, the Lord Mayor said of the mysterious donor:

> We would like to have honoured him publicly as he so deserves but he has so long been so customed 'to do good by stealth and blush to find its fame' that we must respect his wish and offer up our fervent prayer that his life may long be spared to enjoy the consciousness of his own generous instincts.

'The Mystery' is still in use as a place of recreation.

SEPTEMBER 8TH

1939: Liverpool authorities sent out an appeal to women to help run hostels for evacuees. Children had been evacuated out of Liverpool prior to the official declaration of war on Germany on 3 September. Now it was clear that they would be away for some time, the Director of Education asked for any women experienced in the management of households to come forward and assist in areas where the local population were stretched.

On 8 September the *Daily Post* asked those interested to go to the education offices at Sir Thomas Street: 'Women who would be prepared to devote themselves to this work for considerable periods and especially for the duration of the war, would be particularly welcome. In some districts the need is urgent. It is pointed out that certain of the areas are not far distant from Liverpool.'

The Education Department also had to get an idea of how many children hadn't been evacuated, whether it be due to health, holidays or because their parents had decided against it. Reassurance was offered too about the welfare of evacuees, with a head teacher writing from Bangor that: 'She and the other teachers would like Liverpool mothers whose children are there to know that they are happy and healthy and are settling down nicely.'

SEPTEMBER 9TH

1893: Liverpool FC played their first Football League game at Anfield, beating Lincoln City 4-0.

Liverpool had played in the Lancashire League in their inaugural season and were elected to the 2nd Division of the Football League following the demise of Bootle. They won their first fixture 2-0 away to Middlesbrough Ironopolis and a week later Lincoln were the visitors to Anfield. That evening's *Liverpool Echo* reported: 'The weather was somewhat threatening, but there was a capital number of spectators, some four or five thousand being present.'

Two goals from James McBride and one each from Malcolm McVean and Patrick Gordon gave Liverpool the win in a game they never looked likely to lose, being 3-0 up at half time. Liverpool remained unbeaten in the league all season to claim promotion to the 1st Division at the first attempt.

SEPTEMBER 10TH

1935: A motorist caught speeding in the Queensway Tunnel tried to get out of his fine by saying that the Road Traffic Act did not apply there. The following day's *Daily Post and Mercury* reported:

> William Drew, of Village Road, Heswall was summoned for driving a goods motor car in the Queensway Tunnel on August 20th at a speed greater than thirty miles an hour, being the speed specified in the Road Traffic Act 1934, as the maximum speed in relation to a vehicle of that class or description. Mr Joseph Roberts, who defended, contended that the prosecution had been taken under the Road Traffic Act and as the tunnel could not be said to be a highway, the Road Traffic Act did not apply. The essence of a highway, amongst other things, was that it should be a free and uninterrupted method of getting from one place to another for pedestrians and others. Tolls were charged in the tunnel and there was a barrier to pedestrians. The position is exactly the same as if the lorry was driven in a field or private yard.

However, the defence plea cut no ice with the magistrate, who fined Drew £2.

SEPTEMBER 11TH

2001: The people of Liverpool watched in horror as the atrocities at the World Trade Centre in New York were beamed live to their television screens. The following day's *Liverpool Echo* inevitably gave several pages of coverage, including news on Liverpool people caught up near the scene. Sir Paul McCartney was in New York at the time with fiancée Heather Mills, as were local girl band Atomic Kitten (who were preparing to film a video for their single 'You Are').

The Bishop of Liverpool James Jones said: 'Pray for wisdom of the President, pray for stability for the world and pray for the people of America.' Archbishop Patrick Kelly said: 'All we can do is allow the Holy Spirit to make our hearts generous and warm enough to pray for everyone affected in any way.' When the planes struck the Twin Towers, security was increased at Liverpool Airport, docks and government buildings, with police and fire fighters on standby. A Freedom of the City ceremony for Falklands' hero Simon Weston was postponed, but Liverpool FC did play a Champions League match against Portugal's Boavista.

SEPTEMBER 12TH

1766: An auction took place in Liverpool at which slaves were sold. There had been occasional sales in the past but usually involving only one or two slaves, making this sale exceptional. The advert that appeared in Williamson's *Liverpool Advertiser* on 8 September read: 'To be sold at the Exchange Coffee House, Water Street, 12th September at one o'clock precisely, eleven Negroes, imported, per the *Angola*.'

Those sold were likely to have become domestic servants and it was not until 1772 that slaves on English soil were freed.

SEPTEMBER 13TH

1978: Archbishop George Andrew Beck, Archbishop of Liverpool from 1964 to 1976, died.

Prior to coming to Liverpool, Beck was a school headmaster and Bishop of Salford. His time as Archbishop saw the completion of the Metropolitan Cathedral and he also raised the finance for the building of several Catholic schools before being forced to resign due to ill health in 1976. That evening's *Liverpool Echo* carried tributes to him. His successor as Archbishop, Derek Worlock, said: 'He was revered by Clergy and the people for his wonderful example of Christian leadership and fortitude.'

Anglican Bishop David Sheppard said: 'He helped promote the relationship of warmth and trust between the two churches in Liverpool. It has been a privilege to know him both in office and retirement.' Archbishop Beck Catholic Sports College in Fazakerley is named after him.

SEPTEMBER 14TH

1957: Trams were seen on the streets of Liverpool for the last time. The conversion to buses had been taking place over the last ten years, and to mark the passing of the trams a convoy of thirteen set off from the Pier Head at 6.30 p.m. to Bowring Park and then to Edge Lane depot. Nine hundred members of the public were awarded tickets for the last journeys in a ballot, with the very last in the convoy being reserved for VIPs including the Lord Mayor Alderman Frank Cain and local MP Bessie Braddock.

The *Daily Post* reported on 16 September:

> It was the passing of an era, the end of almost a century of trams of various kinds in the city and the citizens did the occasion proud. All of them left in convoy to the strains of Auld Lang Syne played by a band, the wild cheering of the many hundreds of people and the shrieking of the sirens of the Birkenhead ferry and other vessels on the Mersey. Escorting the last tram were five police motor cycle outriders and following it all the way to the depot went a slow procession of hundreds of cars. Doorsteps and windows all along the six mile route were lined with people and cameras clicked from every conceivable angle.

Ironically more than fifty years on trams are back on the streets of some British cities, with Liverpool seeking funding to build three lines.

SEPTEMBER 15TH

1830: The Liverpool & Manchester Railway opened – but the event was tragically overshadowed by the death of local MP William Huskisson.

The line had been six years in the making, with major hurdles to overcome including the tunnel at Olive Mount and marshland at Chat Moss. The world's first passenger railway was a huge event, as the *Liverpool Mercury* reported on 17 September: 'The town itself was never so full of strangers, [and] they poured in from almost all parts of the three kingdoms. All the inns were crowded to overflowing.'

By 9 a.m. on the day of the opening at Crown Street Station, 'The entrance was thronged by the equipages from which the company was alighting. Never was there such an assemblage of rank, wealth, beauty and fashion in this neighbourhood.'

At 11 a.m. a starting gun was fired and the trains set off. After the death of Huskisson in an accident at Parkside, it was decided to continue to Manchester as the crowd there were unruly and impatient. When the train arrived it was pelted with vegetables, and the prime minister, the Duke of Wellington, ordered its immediate return to Liverpool!

September 16th

1956: A service took place at Liverpool Cathedral to commemorate the sixteenth anniversary of the Battle of Britain.

The Second World War battle during the summer and autumn of 1940 was Germany's attempt to gain air superiority over the RAF so it could launch an invasion of England. Just 3,000 pilots from Fighter Command fought the battle, leading Winston Churchill to say, in the House of Commons: 'Never in the field of human conflict has so much been owed by so many to so few.' Five hundred RAF personnel were in the cathedral, with the *Daily Post* reporting the next day:

> Air Marshal Sir Leonard Slatter made the call for remembrance and the congregation knelt as the Ensign was carried to the altar of the war memorial. Canon Giles paid tribute to the pilots on whom he said we were so dependent: 'It was not only on their skill which we were so dependent but their courage.' Following the service there was a march past and the salute was taken on the steps of the cathedral by Air Marshal Sir Bryan V. Reynolds accompanied by Sir Leonard Slatter.

The Battle of Britain continues to be commemorated today on the third Sunday of September.

September 17th

1917: There was good news for Liverpool residents as bread prices were reduced following government subsidies.

There were wheat shortages during the First World War which pushed up the cost of bread, though many also believed that bakers were cashing in as a result by raising prices higher than necessary. The government introduced a Bread Order, stipulating that a loaf must be sold for 9*d*, after coming to an arrangement over subsidies. Despite the fall in prices, the next day's *Liverpool Daily Courier* did have a message for those who may be seeking to buy more, stating:

> This reduction does not mean that bread is more plentiful. The position does not warrant the public to assume that all is well with supplies. There is a world shortage of food and it is the utmost folly to continue eating at the same scale hitherto. The greedy are a menace to the security of this country and to the successful prosecution of the war. Because the bread is cheaper today we must not consume more than we need.

SEPTEMBER 18TH

1854: St George's Hall opened, sixteen years after its foundation stone was laid. The hall was built to hold concerts and events through money raised from public subscription. The foundation stone was laid in 1838, although actual building commenced in 1842. Architect Harvey Lonsdale Elmes passed away during the construction period.

The opening concert involved a performance of the works of Handel. The *Liverpool Mercury*, reporting the following day of the preliminaries, had this to say:

> The Mayor and his party were escorted the whole of the distance by a body of the fire brigade. On alighting from the carriages the party, led by the Mayor, proceeded to the library in the west corridor and joined with members of the Council, where a procession was marshalled. By this time the seats in the body of the hall had become fully occupied. The musical performers had taken their places in the orchestra and as the principal singers made their appearances they were greeted with applause. Precisely at eleven o'clock the procession entered the hall, preceded by the regalia of the Corporation.

After going into decline in the 1980s St George's Hall has now been magnificently restored to its former glory.

SEPTEMBER 19TH

1866: The *Great Eastern* returned to Liverpool after carrying out a telegraph cable laying operation in the Atlantic Ocean. The first Trans-Atlantic telegraph was laid in 1858 but failed after a few weeks. However, funds and better technology were by now in place to lay a new cable from Ireland to Newfoundland, a task the *Great Eastern* set about in July. The operation was finished at Newfoundland on 7 September, and on 20 September the *Liverpool Mercury* reported:

> The *Great Eastern* arrived safely in the River Mersey by yesterday morning's tide. The landing stages were thronged very early with persons anxious to see the great ship after the wonderful accomplishment of the wonderful enterprise of which she has been engaged during the past few weeks. She steamed majestically past the landing stages up the river with the Union Jack flying at the stern, the American Stars and Stripes at the fore, and the Anglo American flag of the Atlantic Telegraph Company at the mainmast. Externally the *Great Eastern* looks very much weather beaten and she will be thoroughly overhauled whilst in port.

SEPTEMBER 20TH

1859: A pub landlord was fined after assaulting a troublesome customer in the street.

Daniel Francis was landlord of the Australian Vaults in Hood Street, which had a dancing saloon attached. The court was told that a Spanish seaman named Valentine got into a quarrel with one of the musicians and they both went out into the street to continue it. Francis went outside and tried to separate them and in the process knocked Valentine down – before kicking him in the face, his boot causing a scar three quarters of an inch deep. The following day's *Liverpool Mercury* reported that the judge acknowledged Valentine had been the cause of a disturbance and Francis had been trying to persuade him to go home, but in causing the injuries that he did had gone too far.

It stated that the judge concluded that: 'He could not help feeling that he was considerably to blame for his excess of violence. He should not inflict so heavy a fine as he should have done if the complainant was not to blame. The defendant must pay 40 shillings plus costs. The fine was paid at once.'

SEPTEMBER 21ST

1929: The *Pageant of Cuckooland* took place at Stanley Park, a play performed in front of 1,200 children.

It took place to celebrate the opening of the Audley Garden, a children's play area developed thanks to the generosity of Southport businessman George Audley, who had also donated the Peter Pan statue to Sefton Park. The *Daily Post and Mercury* reported on 23 September that Audley himself took part in the play, which involved him getting captured by a cuckoo and then pirates. The Lord Mayor and Lady Mayoress also had roles, but it was the capture of Mr Audley by pirates that the children enjoyed the most, 'so that they could boil him and have "boiled Audley" for tea and all because he likes Peter Pan.'

After the play had finished gifts of books, cakes and sweets were distributed to the children and then, in the evening, a crowd of 5,000 attended a further performance prior to a reception for the cast of sixty at the Adelphi hotel.

SEPTEMBER 22ND

1930: Concerns were raised at a meeting of the Liverpool Education Committee over boys visiting a bullfight whilst in Spain. The following day's *Daily Post and Mercury* reported that the boys' visit to the bullfight had been covered in a national newspaper – in which the group gave their opinions of it – and that Mr Hardman, the chair of the committee, didn't see any educational value in it.

However, in response the *Post* reported Alderman Luke Hogan as saying: 'The boys went to a country where bullfighting was the national sport and it was regarded equally as elevating as fox hunting and stag hunting in this country. The boys went to see the customs of the country.'

Another member of the committee, Mr Gordon, backed Mr Hogan saying: 'The boys paid their own expenses and masters sacrificed some of their holidays to accompany them. Every English boy should see at least one bullfight.' As such the discussion was closed by Mr Hardman and they moved on to the next topic, the resignation of a Mr Holt from the committee.

SEPTEMBER 23RD

1983: There was a short-term boost for tunnel users when toll-booth operators walked out en masse to attend a union meeting. The *Liverpool Echo* reported that evening:

> Motorists got a toll free trip through the Birkenhead Tunnel this afternoon after a walkout by toll collectors. At the Wallasey Tunnel tolls were still being collected by automatic booths, with change for those needing it provided by an inspector. The fourteen toll booth operators left their positions at 12.45 p.m. for a union meeting.

Nowadays both tunnels have automatic toll booths so it is unlikely such a bonus will ever be given to motorists again.

SEPTEMBER 24TH

1830: The funeral took place of William Huskisson, the MP for Liverpool (and former member of the Board of Trade) who had tragically been killed during the opening of the Liverpool & Manchester Railway.

Huskisson had been run over by a locomotive as he got out of his carriage at Parkside to speak to the Duke of Wellington. The *Liverpool Mercury* estimated that 60,000 people turned out to see Huskisson's funeral procession travel from the Town Hall to St James Cemetery, where a service was conducted in the oratory before the burial. The *Mercury*'s publication was delayed until 3 p.m. on the day of the funeral, when it described the scene as follows:

> The funeral, which has just terminated, was one of the most extraordinary public spectacles ever witnessed in this country. The windows of every house in the long line of the procession and the roofs of many of them were filled with spectators. Each lamppost had its occupant and the trees in front of the Lyceum were bowed down with persons clinging to every branch. When the Reverend Mr Brooks commenced that part of the funeral service which is delivered at the grave, the hats of thousands of the spectators were instantly removed.

Today his tomb is a main feature of St James' Cemetery, whilst Huskisson Street was also named after him.

SEPTEMBER 25TH

1882: There was a welcome addition to the local hotel scene when Seafield House in Seaforth opened. The following day's *Liverpool Mercury* stated that there had long been a need for a first-class marine hotel. This enterprise, led by ship-owner W. J. Fernie, had 250 bedrooms and also baths, and was set in ten acres of land now occupied by the Seaforth flyover and Port of Liverpool. The following day's *Liverpool Mercury* reported:

> Yesterday the Rt Hon. the Earl of Lathom formally opened a new suite of buildings in connection with Seafield House, which have been erected for the purposes of a hydropathic hotel by a group of Liverpool gentlemen. The band of the 2nd Lancashire Artillery Volunteers played a selection of music in the grounds and several of the visitors engaged in a trial of skill in the archery ground and at the billiard tables of the establishment.

During the night there was a fireworks display watched by thousands, described as 'one of picturesqueness and beauty rarely witnessed in the provinces'.

Unfortunately the venture was not a success and after just two years Seafield House closed and later became a convent, workhouse and government offices before it was demolished in 1970.

SEPTEMBER 26TH

1899: There was an extraordinary demand at the Shakespeare Theatre to see *The Christian*, the latest play by Manx playwright Hall Caine. The play was an adaptation of Caine's best-selling novel of the same name about a young woman trying to live an independent life. The *Liverpool Mercury* described the extraordinary scenes at the box office, reporting the following day:

> A scene of the most unusual character took place yesterday at the Shakespeare Theatre. The majority of people who thronged the theatre hall and footpath were eager to book for Mr Hall Caine's play. A correspondent who has had a wide experience in theatrical matters in Liverpool writes, 'I have witnessed some scenes during our creamy opera season but anything like this rush I have never dreamt of.'

The play did not eventually live up to expectations but Caine continued to be an extremely successful author and was knighted in 1917.

SEPTEMBER 27TH

1924: Liverpool civic dignitaries set off for the French village of Givenchy, where they were to take part in a ceremony handing over a new memorial hall.

After the First World War many English towns and cities adopted places in France. Liverpool provided funds to Givenchy to restore their church and build a new town hall. The *Liverpool Echo* reported that day:

> The little French village that is forever Liverpool will have a new chapter in its history tomorrow with the opening of the hall dedicated by Liverpool in commemoration of the heroes of the Lancashire Division who made immortal history there in the days of the Great War. Liverpool's representatives who are to take part in the ceremonies tomorrow left Victoria Station at 10 a.m. today A Pullman car had been reserved on the Dover express for the accommodation of the party. The party was due to arrive in Lille at 3.39 p.m. Upon reaching the station at Quinchy [*sic*], near Givenchy, at 10.24 on Sunday morning the Liverpool party will be received by parliamentary and civic authorities and will then walk to Liverpool's adopted village, where the Lord Mayor will declare the Memorial Hall open. At noon there will be a luncheon, after which a visit will be paid to the British War Cemetery in Givenchy.

Civic visits continued to Givenchy until the outbreak of the Second World War in 1939.

SEPTEMBER 28TH

1949: Floodlit football came to Merseyside as non-league South Liverpool took on a Nigerian XI at Holly Park in Garston. The match marked the end of a month-long tour by the Nigerians, which had begun on 31 August with a 5-2 win over Crosby side Marine.

The lights at Holly Park were switched on by Lord Mayor Alderman J.J. Cleary, and the *Daily Post* said the next day, 'Except for patches of darkness in the centre of the field the floodlighting proved a success'. In front of a crowd of 13,007, white enamel balls that the players could easily see were used and changed every ten minutes. The Nigerians scored after thirty seconds and were 2-0 up at half time but South fought back to earn a draw. The only downside was an injury to their left back Parr, who was taken to hospital with a broken collar bone.

Holly Park never attracted such a large crowd again in its history and it would be another eight years before Liverpool and Everton installed lights.

SEPTEMBER 29TH

1980: The world's longest play was performed at the Everyman theatre. Neil Oram's epic *The Warp* was acknowledged by the *Guinness Book of Records* and took twenty-two hours to perform, although it was scheduled to be acted out over a period of ten weeks. In previewing the play on 26 September, the *Liverpool Echo* reported:

> It is an idea that has never been tried before on this scale. Artistic director Ken Campbell doesn't believe it is a gamble. 'This is the most sensational, outrageous and moving show I know, it's the funniest thing I've ever seen and there's loads of music in it, so where is the gamble?' asked Ken. 'Each play is complete in itself so you don't have to see every play to know what is going on and enjoy it'. The Warp play cycle dramatizes the adventures of a poet across two decades of the alternative society.

SEPTEMBER 30TH

1874: The Seaman's Orphanage opened in Newsham Park. A group of merchants and shipowners had founded the institution in 1869, using a temporary building in Duke Street. The new building in 1874 was purpose built on land donated by Liverpool Corporation.

The building was opened by the Duke of Edinburgh and the *Liverpool Mercury* issued a rallying call for donations the next day:

> The necessity for such an institution in a port like Liverpool is best shown by the fact that 200 poor children whose fathers perished at sea are already provided for within its walls and at least 100 more are seeking admission. There is so much unrelieved destitution amongst the children of lost sailors that the orphanage even when full will not nearly receive all the cases pressing for admission. The amount required is a mere trifle compared with the wealth represented by the mercantile trade of Liverpool. We look for an immediate and most simple response to the special appeal made by the committee.

In 1886 Queen Victoria visited and it became the Royal Seaman's Orphanage. It closed in 1949 and two years later opened as Park Hospital until its closure in 1988. Despite the closure, the organisation still exists to provide support to families in the city (albeit not by way of accommodation).

OCTOBER 1ST

1985: Riots erupted in Toxteth for the second time in four years. Trouble started during the evening rush hour, when motorists were dragged from their cars which were then set alight on Princes Road. It followed angry scenes at court earlier in the day when four men were remanded in custody at a hearing attended by up to 100 people.

Disturbances continued throughout the night, with stones being thrown at cars and police until an uneasy peace settled in the early hours. Media crews were also targeted, with one television crew having to surrender £20,000 worth of equipment. The following day's *Daily Post* reported:

> Toxteth was the scene of angry clashes last night as stone throwing mobs confronted police in full riot gear. Hundreds of youths lined the streets as armoured police vans moved in to disperse the youths. A sergeant suffered a fractured jaw when hit by a missile and two policewomen were taken to hospital after being cut by flying glass when a brick was thrown through their van window.

Thankfully the night's rioting was a one-off and there was no repeat of the week-long riots of 1981.

OCTOBER 2ND

1981: The funeral took place of Bill Shankly, who was manager of Liverpool FC from 1959 to 1974, taking them from the 2nd Division to becoming one of the most feared teams in Europe.

Shankly died of a heart attack in Broadgreen Hospital at the age of sixty-seven. For his funeral, 200 leading figures from the game converged on Anfield where they were taken to St Mary's church in West Derby on four special coaches. That evening's *Liverpool Echo* reported on the sad day:

> Leaden skies matched the mood of a city as Bill Shankly's funeral took place. Some people were openly weeping. A small boy, his Liverpool scarf wrapped soddenly round his neck, cried as the coffin was carried into church. The church resounded to *Amazing Grace* – a hymn the Kop has adapted in its own inimitable way in tribute to Shanks. The reading, from Corinthians and Hebrews, was given by Liverpool Chairman John Smith and the address by former Liverpool star Ian St John. He said, 'We were honoured to have Bill Shankly mould us from boys into men'. The service ended with that Kopite anthem *You'll Never Walk Alone*. Tears welled in many eyes as the pall bearers carried Shankly's coffin out of the church to the tune of that Kopite hymn.

Shankly was then cremated at Anfield Crematorium, within sight of his beloved football ground of the same name.

OCTOBER 3RD

1788: The King's Dock opened. The dock was built at a cost of £25,000, extending the system south and being built on the site of many shipyards which were demolished. It was named after the reigning monarch at the time, George III. The opening and coverage were very low key, with *Williamson's Advertiser* giving it just a paragraph in its edition of 6 October: 'On Friday the new dock, the King's Dock, at the south end of town, was opened and the water let into it when the *Amphitrite*, Greenland ship, Captain Pagan commander, entered it.'

After being filled in following its closure in 1972, and acting as a car park for many years, in 2008 the dock was given a new lease of life with the building of the Echo Arena, BT Convention Centre, hotels, apartments and restaurants.

OCTOBER 4TH

1871: St Chad's church in Kirkby was consecrated. The church, paid for by the Earl of Sefton, took over two years to build as a stonemason's strike delayed construction. The consecration was carried out by the Bishop of Chester following a communion service in the old chapel it was replacing. The *Liverpool Mercury* reported the next day:

> The public were admitted by ticket and there was a very large congregation, the edifice being filled. At the commencement the Bishop was received by the Rev. Canon Gray, Vicar of Kirkby. The petition praying the Bishop to consecrate the church was presented by the Vicar to His Lordship. The Bishop, having declared his readiness to comply with the prayer of the petition, proceeded to consecrate and dedicate the church. The procession of clergy then moved from the communion table to the west end of the church and back again, where the deed of conveyance was presented to the Bishop, who having said the prescribed prayers directed the sentence of consecration to be read, which was done by his secretary. The usual service at Morning Prayer then followed.

St Chad's today stands in the middle of a much larger community than it was first built for.

OCTOBER 5TH

1937: Liverpool's housing improvement programme took a major step forward with the official opening of Myrtle Gardens in Myrtle Street.

The scheme comprised of 344 flats, 290 of which consisted of 2 or 3 bedrooms. There were also gardens, recreation areas and playgrounds for children. Similar schemes were also being developed at the St Andrew's Gardens off London Road and Gerard Gardens in Vauxhall.

Minister of Health Sir Kingsley Wood conducted the opening, the *Daily Post* reporting the next day:

> Sir Kingsley's arrival was greeted by cheering from tenants of the occupied flats, who crowded the balconies facing the dais erected for the occasion and crowded in hundreds on the ground level. During a tour of the tenements Sir Kingsley opened the playgrounds by unlocking the gate and entering with one of the scores of children who were jumping with eagerness to get to the swings.

After trying out the swings himself, the minister praised the local housing programme, saying that Liverpool was becoming much richer in its provision of new dwellings.

During the 1970s Myrtle Gardens fell into disrepair, but in the 1980s two of the three blocks were renovated and re-named Minster Court.

OCTOBER 6TH

1973: Liverpool's last greyhound track, the White City in Lower Breck Road, closed.

The opening of the Breck Park track in Clubmoor in 1927 had led to a surge in popularity, with White City being one of three more to be built in the city, but all these tracks would be gone within fifty years. Around 700 people attended the final meeting at White City, which was held on a Saturday night. The *Daily Post* reported on 8 October:

> There was no ceremony to mark the passing. 'We just want to go as quietly as possible', said the manager Mr Edward Baines, now retiring after 45 years in the business. Following the closure of the stadium the eighty company-owned greyhounds are being moved to other tracks and much of the stadium equipment is being sold.

St Margaret's junior school now stands on the site.

OCTOBER 7TH

1913: A religious group member's jealousy led to a double murder and suicide.

The Positivists worshipped at the Temple of Humanity in Upper Parliament Street. Jealous of the relationship between two other members, Paul Gaze and Mary Crompton, William McDonald shot them both dead at their homes in Grove Street and Bedford Street South and then shot himself. He had earlier shot and seriously wounded Richard Roberts, who had introduced him to the Positivists.

On 9 October the *Liverpool Daily Courier* called it 'the most appalling crime ever perpetrated in Liverpool.... Civilised community members must shudder to think that a young man can escape the vigilance of the police and commit two successive murders and an attempted murder in three different houses and finally commit suicide.'

The *Courier* said of the scene at 81 Bedford Street South: 'Mary Crompton was found lying on the floor with a revolver shot wound in the temple and a glance at her figure quickly assured officers that life was extinct. In the same room McDonald was found lying on the floor suffering serious injuries to the head.'

McDonald died three hours later in hospital. After the killings, the Temple of Humanity slowly disbanded.

OCTOBER 8TH

1886: A harvest thanksgiving service took place at St Nicholas' church. Traditionally held on the nearest full moon to the autumn equinox, in this year it occurred on a Friday. The following day's *Liverpool Daily Courier* reported:

Canon Blencowe gave an able and appropriate address from Galatians vi 7 and 8. The musical arrangements were under the direction of Mr Ashlin and were most excellent, the singing being very fine and the accompaniment of the talented organist was a treat to hear. The decorations were very beautiful and to good taste. The ladies who assisted this were Mrs Sillitoe and Mrs Winter, who did the pews and windows; Miss Batty the font; Mrs and Miss Kempster and Miss Goulborne the altar rails; the Misses Doo and Misses Burff the choir stalls and pulpit; Mrs Woodcock, Miss Kilshaw and Miss Olds the reading desk and lectern; Miss Storey, Miss Armstrong and Miss Porter the pillars; and Miss Anderson the texts. These decorations will remain in the church tomorrow (Sunday) when there will be a special sermon on behalf of the Society for the Preparation of the Gospel.

OCTOBER 9TH

1950: The Liverpool & District Chrysanthemum Society opened a three-day show.

The show was held at the Gaumont Cinema in Allerton Road and opened by local comedian Billy Matchett. The *Daily Post* reported the next day: 'There were over 200 entries and the standard was exceptionally high for the time of year. Miss Sorby of Wirral won the Gaumont Theatre Cup for the best exhibit in the show. Gold medals for trade exhibits were awarded to Mr Boardman of Moreton and Mr Alexander of Lee Park.'

In all nine prizes were awarded, with the furthest winner having travelled from Formby to take part, winning the category of 'the best bowl of chrysanthemums arranged for effect'.

OCTOBER 10TH

1982: The first episode of *Boys From the Black Stuff* was aired on BBC2. Former schoolteacher Alan Bleasdale's *The Black Stuff*, following a group of Liverpool tarmac layers on a job in Middlesbrough, was shown as a *Play for Today* in January 1980. Nearly three years down the line the series focused on the fortunes of the gang, now unemployed and living in a city where jobs were nearly impossible to come by. The first episode aired at 10.10 p.m. on a Sunday night. The *Liverpool Echo*'s television listing said, 'The celebrated tarmac gang are back – to a city without work in a series of five screen plays made on Merseyside.' A brief feature with the writer said: 'Bleasdale sees it as a tribute to the spirit of his native Liverpool but admits that it is an even bleaker picture than he realised when he wrote it.'

The series, which focused on the hopelessness and despair of being out of work, was such a talking point that it was shown again on BBC1 just nine weeks after it finished. It won the British Academy Award for Best Drama Serial and in 2007 came second in a Channel 4 production 'Best 50 Television Dramas' as voted for by industry professionals.

OCTOBER 11TH

1901: A prisoner from Liverpool made a daring jump for freedom when he leapt from an express train. The prisoner was being escorted from Liverpool to Ludlow, which required a change of train at Crewe. It was from this express that the dangerous leap was made. The *Liverpool Daily Courier* reported the next day:

An alleged notorious thief and burglar was in the custody of Sergeant Williams of the Ludlow police, who had brought him from Liverpool. The express had attained a high rate of speed when the prisoner suddenly opened the carriage door and leapt from the train. Without hesitation his custodian pluckily followed him. Both fell heavily to the permanent way and were in a dazed condition, the policeman being badly confused about the head. The incident was witnessed by several railway officials but before they could reach the spot where the men lay the prisoner had recovered from the shock and dashed away, hotly pursued by Sergeant Williams. An exciting chase ensued but the fugitive had by this time got a good lead. He made a desperate effort to climb the embankment which leads to the new railway extension. In another second he would have been over but by a tremendous effort his follower managed to clutch him by the heel and both dropped heavily. Neither prisoner nor officer could speak for several minutes.

OCTOBER 12TH

1922: An Aigburth resident failed to secure the damages he hoped for against his neighbour who, he claimed, had damaged his rose trees and an ornamental vase.

That night's *Evening Express* reported that George Henry Hewitt of Woodland Road was seeking £7 in compensation from George Dolman of Cromer Road, stating that a tree felled by Dolman had broken three rose trees and an ornamental vase. However, Dolman produced evidence that the rose trees had in fact bloomed better than ever since the accident and the vase was not broken, but simply needed lifting back into position. Hewitt had refused his offer to put things right.

The judge decided that some damages were appropriate nonetheless due to the inconvenience caused, the *Express* reporting: 'His Honour said the pecuniary claim was very much exaggerated and he thought £2 would be sufficient compensation. Judgement was given for the Plaintiff of two pounds and one guinea for the costs of witnesses.'

OCTOBER 13TH

1948: Liverpool welcomed forty delegates from the Commonwealth of Nations who were taking a tour of the city before attending the bi-annual Commonwealth Parliamentary Conference in London the following week.

The visitors included delegates from Australia, New Zealand, India, Pakistan and Windward Islands, who arrived in Liverpool after first visiting Manchester. Whilst in the city they were taken on a tour of the Dunlop rubber factory in Speke, Dock Board offices, Kirkby housing estate and Liverpool Cathedral. The *Evening Express* reported that night that Liverpool 'had a united nations assembly on its own doorstep today' and that they 'saw many aspects of its activity'.

OCTOBER 14TH

1920: The *Evening Express* reported a curious case. On this day three customers were asked to leave a Liverpool restaurant after they refused to stand when a band played the National Anthem, angering others present:

A remarkable and exciting scene took place last night in a well-known and popular Liverpool restaurant. In the restaurant mentioned is an orchestra, which each evening plays the National Anthem near closing time, when everyone stands until the strains die away. Last evening however three individuals were seen to deliberately remain seated, an action that at once provoked angry remarks from other diners. One gentleman protested against such conduct which he regarded as an insult to the rest of the company who had acted as Britishers. Several other gentlemen joined in expressing themselves over the matter and soon the whole of those present showed signs of anger and demanded the removal of the offending trio. The manager requested the men to leave the restaurant, which they did in a very subdued fashion, their departure being accompanied by rousing cheers for the King and Prince of Wales and cries of, 'We want no Bolsheviks in Liverpool'.

OCTOBER 15TH

1866: The New Prince of Wales Theatre opened with a performance of the opera *Faust*.

It was Liverpool's largest theatre to date and the *Liverpool Mercury* believed it was something the town could be proud of: 'The architectural beauties of Lime Street will have no cause to be ashamed by this handsome stranger. The size of the building at present somewhat dwarfs those adjoining but when the proposed new railway arrangements are completed a line of fine structures will be carried right along Lime Street.' The *Mercury* described the theatre as 'likely to prove one of the most attractive, complete and comfortable theatres in the provinces. Of the opening performance itself, it said:

> The grand inauguration of the theatre was something to be remembered. Enthusiasm on the part of the audience and efficiency of the artistes were the grand characteristics of the whole performance. Every seat in the capacious house was occupied and the gorgeous variety of colours produced by the ladies' dresses, relieved by the more sober costume of the gentlemen, gave an animation to the whole scene of the most pleasing description.

In 1867 the theatre was re-named the Royal Alexandra and in the 1920s it was demolished to make way for the Empire.

OCTOBER 16TH

1902: Viscount Kitchener, commander of British forces in the Boer War (which had ended the previous May), was presented with a personalised gift by a storekeeper when he visited Liverpool:

Mr E. Cohen, Standard Umbrella Stores, 69 Church Street, on the occasion of Viscount Kitchener's visit, presented His Lordship with a handsome walking stick. It is a partridge cane with an ivory claw handle on which a lion is carved. It is gold crested, with Viscount Kitchener's crest, and bears a suitable inscription. Mr Cohen has received a letter from the Earl of Derby acknowledging the receipt of the stick and stated that His Lordship had handed it to Viscount Kitchener, who expressed pleasure at receiving the present.

(Liverpool Daily Courier)

OCTOBER 17TH

1886: A seaman was killed when he fell overboard from a vessel in Clarence Dock. The *Liverpool Daily Courier* reported the next day under what would now be seen as an extremely insensitive headline of 'EXCITING SCENE AT CLARENCE DOCK':

An incident which caused considerable excitement yesterday afternoon occurred at about a quarter past three o'clock at the entrance to Clarence Dock. Whilst the SS *Lara*, belonging to the Waterford Steamship Company, was leaving the river for the purpose of entering Clarence Dock a seaman named John Connors was engaged passing a rope from the starboard side of the vessel to the pier head when he fell overboard into the river. Lifebuoys were immediately thrown out to him and every endeavour was made to rescue the man. But as there was a strong ebb tide running at the time it was too powerful for him and he failed to reach the lifebuoys.

A dock gateman divested himself of his coat and his boots, jumped into the river and swam to the spot where he saw Connors fall in but his gallant effort was of no avail as the poor fellow had disappeared. The body had not been recovered last night. The dock gateman was taken to the Collingwood Dock receiving house where he changed his clothes and left apparently none the worse for his courageous exertions.

OCTOBER 18TH

1864: The Grand Southern Bazaar, a fundraising event to raise money for wounded Confederate prisoners and their families, was opened at St George's Hall.

Although Britain was neutral in the American Civil War, the merchants of Liverpool were very much on the side of the Confederates and this event was raised to provide some relief to prisoners. It involved stalls named after Southern states selling goods and having prize raffles. The opening day was a profitable one, the *Liverpool Mercury* reporting the following day:

> If the next three days upon which the bazaar continues furnishes anything like a proportionate contribution the next result for the treasury will be something very handsome representing several thousand pounds sterling which will go a long way to provide comforts and necessaries for the sick and wounded men who have lost liberty in fighting for the Southern cause. To the making up of this goodly sum a large number of fashionable visitors with well filled purses contributed. From the opening of the bazaar at noon until its closure at ten the floor of the hall was thronged.

The event went on to raise £20,000 – the equivalent of £12 million today.

OCTOBER 19TH

1781: British troops surrendered at Yorktown, Virginia. It brought an end the involvement in the American War of Independence of Liverpool's Lieutenant Colonel Banastre Tarleton.

Tarleton, an officer serving under overall commander Lord Cornwallis, was the son of John Tarleton, Mayor in 1764. Lord Cornwallis accepted the terms of the surrender in a letter to General Washington on 18 October, which said, 'I agree to open a treaty of capitulation upon the basis of the garrisons of York and Gloucester, including seamen, being prisoners of war.'

In August 1780 Tarleton had written to his brother from Camp Camden, South Carolina. The letter contained details of his military involvement:

> I had the honour of a great command in the first actions, [and] the last was wholly entrusted to me. I received a slight wound in the first, did not require dressing. Two days afterward I fought with every honour my best friend would wish. Lord Cornwallis's letters will name the circumstances of the defeat of Horatio Gates.

In December 1781 Tarleton returned to Liverpool. He went on to be an MP from 1790 to 1812.

OCTOBER 20TH

1938: The funeral took place of Edward Stanley, Secretary of State for Dominion Affairs and heir to the earldom of Derby, who died aged just forty-four. Stanley had only been a member of the Cabinet for five months at the time of his premature death. The following day's *Daily Post* reported the funeral, which was conducted by the Bishop of Liverpool:

> Touching scenes at Knowsley parish church yesterday marked the funeral of Lord Stanley. It was attended only by relatives and tenants but simultaneously memorial services were held at Westminster Abbey, Liverpool and Manchester cathedrals. The coffin was carried to the graveside by gamekeepers, foresters and men from the building yard at Knowsley Hall.

Of the memorial at Liverpool Cathedral, the *Post* said:

> The service afforded striking evidence, were it needed, of the sure place held by Lord Stanley in the affection and goodwill of Merseyside. It expressed through prayer and praise a sense of personal and community loss, a thankfulness that Lord Stanley, though cut off in the prime of his manhood, had lived long enough to accomplish so much. There have been many memorial services in the cathedral to worthy men but it is difficult to recall one at which the note of regret was deeper than that which marked this one.

OCTOBER 21ST

1915: The recruitment drive for war service was again stepped up in Liverpool. The First World War had been going on for a year, and although conscription had yet to be introduced, Lord Derby was actively trying to recruit as many men of fighting age as possible. The *Evening Express* reported that evening that up to 75,000 letters signed by Lord Derby were being prepared to send out over the next few days. Of those who had signed up over the last week, the *Evening Express* said:

> The last seven days show a remarkable improvement upon previous weeks in Liverpool and a rapid increase commencing with Sunday. The large majority of these men are resident in Liverpool but there are many who although resident across the water or in Bootle or Seaforth make up their minds to join whilst at business. Without allowing their ardour time to cool they make a bee line for the recruiting office and transact the business of attestation and undergo the medical examination straight away. Others are brought from the highways and by-ways as well as from the high seas, the system of recruiting officers visiting steamers arriving in Liverpool having been consistently carried out.

The following January, conscription was introduced for all single men aged eighteen to forty-one.

OCTOBER 22ND

1926: A British Enka Co. artificial silk factory opened in Aintree, part of a drive to bring more varied employment opportunities to the region, especially for women. The Lord Mayor himself turned a silver key which allowed viscose to find its way to a spinning machine and make the first artificial silk in Liverpool. That evening's *Liverpool Echo* reported that Sir Henry Strakosch, chairman of the British Enka Co., said: 'When the works reach their full production, towards the middle of next year, they would bring added prosperity to Liverpool by giving employment to several thousand operatives in a healthy industry producing an article of quality.' The Lord Mayor said:

> I am very pleased to be able to come to this factory not only because it is a new industry in our midst and not only because it is a sign of development and progress, but because it is the beginning of what I hope will be better things in our endeavour to overcome unemployment. This factory is a grand beginning to what I anticipate a great future.

The factory, later known as Courtaulds after a takeover, was closed in the 1980s and a retail park stands on its site.

OCTOBER 23RD

1954: The centenary of the St Francis Xavier parish schools was celebrated in Everton.

SFX, as the church was and remains commonly known, founded the schools to provide education to poor Catholic children in the neighbourhood.

The *Daily Post* reported of the centenary on 25 October:

The centenary on Saturday of St Francis Xavier's parish schools, Haigh Street, Liverpool, was observed with a Solemn High Mass of thanksgiving in the church of St Francis Xavier, attended by 1,800 children of the schools. Celebrant of the mass was the Reverend H. Waterhouse with the Rev. T. O'Neill as Deacon and the Rev. B Weatherhead as Sub-Deacon.

OCTOBER 24TH

1983: Job centres were besieged as Liverpool City Council advertised for 600 new workers. The recruitment had been announced the week before and the *Liverpool Echo* reported that evening of the scenes at job centres:

> The jobs bonanza caused early morning queues at several centres and at Old Swan, one of the busiest, the first man taken off the dole queue had been there by 4.30 a.m. At one stage 500 people were queuing at Old Swan: 'it was like something you see on TV when they do a documentary about unemployment, only this was for real, you could see the hope in people's eyes,' said one man. Other offices were crowded as workers young and old tried to cash in on one of the vacancies. Almost all of the vacancies released this morning had been snapped up within a couple of hours.

OCTOBER 25TH

1978: A service of thanksgiving and dedication attended by Queen Elizabeth II took place at Liverpool Cathedral to mark its completion, some seventy-four years after the foundation stone had been laid. The service involved an unveiling of a completion stone by the Queen and in the spirit of ecumenicalism the city's Catholic Archbishop, Derek Worlock, also played a part.

After arriving by royal train the Queen had lunch at the Town Hall before attending the service. The *Daily Post* reported the next day:

> The service at the cathedral, bathed in television lights and glowing with colour provided the pageantry. More than 2,500 guests from all walks of life attended the magnificent ceremony. In the presence of Elizabeth II, whose great grandfather Edward VII had laid the foundation stone, Liverpool inherited the world's fifth largest cathedral, the first mother church in the northern provinces since the Reformation. No words can adequately convey the feeling of thanksgiving.

After the service the Queen made a surprise appearance on the balcony of the Town Hall before mingling with crowds in Castle Street. The royal party then headed to Speke Airport for a flight to London.

OCTOBER 26TH

1814: St George's church in Everton, the first cast-iron church in the world, was consecrated. Construction of the church, designed by Thomas Rickman, began in April 1813 and although its outer shell was stone, the interior and roof were made from cast iron. The *Liverpool Mercury* reported on 28 October:

> The ceremony was performed on Wednesday morning at half past eleven o'clock by the Right Reverend Father in God, George Henry, Lord Bishop of this Diocese, who arrived for that purpose at the home of James Atherton, Esq, of Everton Lodge, and proceeded immediately to the church. The service was read by the Rev. Wm. Godwin of Walton; afterwards an excellent sermon was preached by the Rev. R.P. Buddicorn, Minister of the said church. The consecration and service were not over until after three o'clock. A very handsome cold collation was prepared on the occasion at the St George's hotel, adjoining the church, for the Bishop, Ministry and proprietors. A more respectable table was never witnessed. The wines were of the first quality and the whole did great credit to Mr Dale the landlord.

St George's church is still going strong today and is a Grade I listed building.

OCTOBER 27TH

1958: The annual poppy appeal was launched, with the Lord Mayor of Liverpool buying the first one in the city. The *Liverpool Echo* reported that evening:

First customers at the Poppy Shop, Leece Street when it opened today were the president of the Poppy Day Appeal, the Lord Mayor of Liverpool (Alderman Harry Livermore) and the Lady Mayoress. They each bought a double buttonhole of silk poppies – the Lord Mayor receiving his from Mrs T.H. Hough, president of the Ladies of the Inner Wheel who are running the poppy shop as a team and the Lady Mayoress getting hers from Miss Maud Carpenter, vice president of the Appeal. At the same time the Lord Mayor ordered a large wreath of the poppies which he will place on the cenotaph in the centre of Liverpool on Poppy Day itself, November 8th. According to Miss May Wright, who has organised the Poppy Shop scheme for the past 32 years, as much as £400 is expected from the sale of wreaths and buttonholes from the shop alone. This appeal last year brought in from all sources more than £7,000 and the target this year is £8,000.

OCTOBER 28TH

1858: The salary of the Mayor of Liverpool was brought into question by a reader of the *Liverpool Mercury*. The paper published a letter written by somebody calling himself 'Anti-Humbug' which said:

I read in the *Times* a few days ago that at a meeting of the Newcastle Town Council recently it was resolved by a large majority to abolish the Mayor's salary and that in future only the 'legitimate expenses' are to be allowed. Surely this has not escaped the notice of Mr Gladstone or some of the advocates of retrenchment in our present corporate expenditure. Liverpool is one of only three towns in the country where an allowance is made to the Mayor. It is a stigma on the wealthy class in this town to suppose that no-one could be found to fill what ought to be considered an honourable post without receiving in hard cash the 'quid pro quo'. It is hoped therefore that someone will have sufficient courage at the election of the new Mayor to move that the allowance of £2,000 (or whatever it is) be not made in the future. Having lost a considerable portion of our corporate income we must adjust our expenditure to the altered circumstances. To avoid a heavy borough rate a very large reduction must at once be made elsewhere. Here is an excellent way of making a beginning.

OCTOBER 29TH

1916: The Liverpool Jewish Literary Society moved into a new home opposite the Princes Road Synagogue.

The society had been formed in 1906 with the aim of expressing Judaism and Jewish heritage through the English language. The new building was paid for by the Benas family, who were local Jewish bankers. The *Daily Post and Mercury* reported the following day:

> Greetings and good wishes were sent to the inaugural gathering, at which Mr Bertram Benas occupied the presidential chair. Sir Edward Russell, who was accompanied by Lady Russell, was the principal speaker at the meeting. Sir Edward affirmed that almost everything that was good came through literature and he confirmed that the great religion of the Jewish race had been the foundation of the religion of the world. Sir Edward was cordially thanked for his address on the motion of Mr Lionel Collins.

The literary society remained in existence until 1936.

OCTOBER 30TH

1863: American Congregationalist clergyman Henry Ward Beecher was welcomed by the Liverpool Emancipation Society. Beecher, a staunch Abolitionist, was invited to a special breakfast on the morning of his return to America, where the Civil War was on-going, following a tour of Britain. The *Liverpool Mercury* reported the next day that the chairman of the emancipation society told those present:

> It gives me great honour to provide occasion on which Henry Beecher will address an English audience. I feel that I may thank him in your name and in the name of the friends of emancipation for the ability with which he has advocated the cause of liberty during his stay in England.

Beecher, in beginning his address, declared:

> Although this is a festive scene, it is with feelings of sadness and solemnity that I stand in your midst, for the hours are numbered that I am to be with you and the ship is waiting that I trust will bear me safely to my homeland. Already I have been to the full impressed with these sentiments of reverence and love of romance which attach to these memories.

The Civil war ended two years later, and when Beecher died in 1887, a day of mourning was declared in Brooklyn.

OCTOBER 31ST

1946: Schoolchildren attended one of a series of free concerts given by the Royal Liverpool Philharmonic Orchestra. Altogether eighteen concerts were being organised, allowing for over 30,000 children to enjoy the performances. That night's *Evening Express* revealed:

More than 4,000 children from secondary modern schools in the city attended the two concerts given at the Philharmonic Hall today by Liverpool Philharmonic Orchestra, conducted by Reginald Jacques. The children listened attentively and appreciatively to works by Beethoven, Mozart, Tchaikovsky and other composers. They displayed particular interest in explanations of the music, given by Dr Jacques.

NOVEMBER 1ST

1873: A Vauxhall man murdered his mother in a senseless and unprovoked attack. The murder, described by the *Liverpool Mercury* on 3 November as 'the most horrible of its character ever committed in Liverpool' occurred at 30 Chisenhale Street. Thomas Corrigan, a twenty-three-year-old casual dock porter with a history of assaulting police, set about his mother with his fists, feet, belt and a knife because she hadn't made him anything to eat. Other household members, including his father and lodgers, were too terrified to intervene and when police arrived he told them 'she had fallen down the stairs' and died suddenly. The *Mercury* reported Corrigan's arrest: 'He was taken to the Bridewell and when it was found that his mother was dead and he was charged with murder he replied, "No sir, you are wrong. Who can prove that?" The prisoner, who was perfectly sober when taken into custody and seemed entirely unimpressed by the horrible nature of his crime, will be brought before Mr Raffles, the Stipendiary Magistrate.'

Corrigan was hanged for his crime, the sentencing judge remarking on the enormity of killing somebody he was bound to love and cherish.

NOVEMBER 2ND

1982: The first episode of the Channel 4 soap opera *Brookside*, set in the Liverpool suburb of West Derby, was aired. The soap opera was one of the new channel's flagship shows and filmed in a real life cul-de-sac, with the interior of houses being used as sets, offices and make-up rooms. The *Liverpool Echo*'s television page for that evening said:

> All eyes will be on Channel 4 tonight. And the programme creating most curiosity on Merseyside is *Brookside* (8.00), the new Liverpool based soap opera that puts the emphasis on realism. A lot of hopes are riding on *Brookside*: Channel 4 see it as one of their hopes of winning a popular audience.

The following evening, under the headline '*BROOKSIDE* KICKS OFF WITH A RUMPUS', the *Echo* reported that the show's top director had quit after just three months due to the amount of bad language. The *Echo* itself said: 'It contained one or two "bloodys" and some choice Liverpool expressions that could have offended some people, but seemed appropriate to the characters.'

Brookside reached its peak in the late 1980s and early '90s but after several years of falling viewing figures the last episode was broadcast in 2003.

NOVEMBER 3RD

1903: Canon Thomas Major Lester died of bronchitis. Born in Fulham in 1829, he came to Liverpool in 1853 where he became a curate at St Mary's church in Kirkdale. In all of his time in Liverpool he lived in Netherfield Road, witnessing immense social change. He believed that children who were unclothed and unfed were more liable to have their minds poisoned and he set up the Major Street Ragged schools and Kirkdale Child Charity. The schools provided not just shelter and food, but training in skills to help obtain employment.

The *Liverpool Daily Courier* reported of his death the following day: 'Throughout Liverpool much regret will be felt at the death of the Rev. Canon Thomas Major Lester who passed away at his residence, 294 Netherfield Road, yesterday. A prominent figure in the religious, educational and philanthropist life of this city has been removed.'

Major Lester School was named after him, although in the late 1990s this became Hope Valley following a merger.

NOVEMBER 4TH

1912: At a meeting of Little Woolton (Gateacre) Urban District Council, it was decided not to make public the details of the suggested terms for its incorporation into Liverpool.

The issue had been covered in the press, but as Liverpool had laid out terms to the village, 6 miles south of the city centre, a month earlier, some councillors felt all details should be made public. However, others believed as the council hadn't yet discussed the terms they should remain private. The *Liverpool Daily Courier* reported the next day:

> Mr T. H. Cookson expressed the opinion that in view of the fact that there had been a certain amount of discussion in the newspapers upon the incorporation subject, the public should know the terms. Mr G. Dale remarked that they were not yet in a position to let the public know. The Chairman said that Liverpool had only partly covered the ground and the matter was not yet ripe for public discussion. Mr Cookson said that he did not suggest a public discussion, merely that the public should know the terms. Mr W. H. Cochran said it would not be right to put the matter before the public or even to disclose it outside the council, as it was still at the preliminary stage. It was decided that the question should be considered in private.

Gateacre was absorbed into Liverpool in 1913.

NOVEMBER 5TH

1983: St Andrew's church in Rodney Street was severely damaged by fire. Built in 1823 for Scottish Presbyterians, the church had been closed since 1975 but was to be converted into a new library by Liverpool Polytechnic.

On this Bonfire Night it was the most high-profile fire in the region, the *Daily Post* reporting on 7 November:

> One of Liverpool's listed buildings was almost destroyed by fire at the weekend. The fire, which is being treated as arson, severely damaged the derelict St Andrew's church in Rodney Street, a Grade II listed building. The fire service has said that around 80 per cent of the church was severely damaged after the call was received by the fire service at 7.15 p.m. on Saturday and the remainder of the crew were still damping down the building yesterday afternoon. Two firemen were slightly injured fighting the blaze, they were taken to hospital but released after treatment. Firework wielding vandals are believed to be responsible.

The church has remained out of use since, but in 2012 work started on converting it into student accommodation.

November 6th

1865: The CSS *Shenandoah* arrived in the River Mersey and surrendered – the last act of the American Civil War. The *Shenandoah* had raided Union ships off Alaska after the war ended, the Captain claiming not to have known that hostilities had ended. Knowing he faced execution if he landed at an American port, the ship sailed across the Pacific and eventually towards Liverpool. The following day's *Liverpool Mercury* reported on its arrival and subsequent surrender to the British navy:

> Considerable excitement was caused yesterday morning by the report that the Confederate cruiser *Shenandoah* was passed at eight o'clock by the steamer *Douglas*, apparently waiting for high water. Captain Waddell took a pilot on board and desired the pilot to take his ship alongside one of Her Majesty's vessels of war, if there were any in port. The *Shenandoah* was taken up the river and moored alongside the Donegal. Soon after the surrender of the vessel Captain Waddell and several of the officers and crew went ashore.

Despite appeals from US authorities, the British government refused to hand over any of the *Shenandoah*'s crew.

NOVEMBER 7TH

1960: A mock US presidential election in Liverpool gave John F. Kennedy a resounding victory.

Members of the English Speaking Union met at the Strand Hotel to debate the issues facing the American electorate the following day. Mary Senior, a civic design student from New York, secured victory for Kennedy by eight-eight votes to forty-nine. The *Daily Post* told all the following day:

> Despite the superior debating skill of Dr Douglas Verney, lecturer in political science at the university and well known expert in American politics, he could gain only 49 votes for Vice-President Nixon. Questions from the audience of 150 ranged widely over foreign affairs and religious and colour prejudices. Miss Senior claimed that America's choice was between bringing intelligence or belligerence to bear on relations with Soviet Russia, while Dr Verney asked who would vote for higher taxes. Both spokesmen agreed that the great imponderable in this issue was the religious issue. The Democrats feared the silent bigot; the Republicans felt that many Americans might vote for a Catholic President to show the world that they were free from prejudice. How accurately has this well informed group in Liverpool predicted voting in America?

The real election was a much more close-run thing, Kennedy winning with 49.7 per cent of the vote to Nixon's 49.5 per cent.

NOVEMBER 8TH

1928: There were cheers at Liverpool Assizes as a Liverpool labourer was cleared of the murder of a German tailor's presser.

Maurice McCormack was charged with the murder of John Seman, who had been having an affair with his wife. The crime scene was at Iden Street, which stood on the site of the Royal Liverpool University Hospital. During the trial the court heard how Seman suffered a knife wound to the neck. However, McCormack maintained that, although a scuffle took place between the two men, it was Seman who had a knife. He himself had not struck any blows or handled the knife, and Seman had walked away – apparently uninjured – from the scuffle.

That evening's *Evening Express* reported that the jury took just fourteen minutes to find McCormack not guilty, and that on leaving the dock:

> McCormack was kissed by an elderly woman and was embraced by two men who were trembling with emotion. The cheering in the court was immediately suppressed but when the verdict became known to the crowd outside there was a further demonstration of approval McCormack left the court, his face covered by a handkerchief.

NOVEMBER 9TH

1946: The countdown to Christmas started as Father Christmas took a ferry across the River Mersey before taking temporary residence in the Lewis's store. That evening's *Evening Express* reported:

Father Christmas came to town this morning. He arrived at Liverpool landing stage by boat travelling in the SS *Santa Claus* – the Woodside ferry boat *Hinderton*. Long before the boat was due to arrive the pier head was a seething mass of excited children accompanied by their parents. Each of the small red refuse bins attached to the side of the standards held a child who from the vantage point screamed to the less fortunate companions, 'the boat is coming – there he is, there he is!' Meanwhile mothers, fathers, big brothers and big sisters hoisted smaller children onto their shoulders to catch a sight of the red cloaked bewhiskered figure. Up the gangway walked Father Christmas and there a famous old stage coach the *Ventura* waited for the distinguished guest. Father Christmas waved his hand and after slinging his bag of presents into the coach sat beside the driver and off they moved. They followed a tour of the city via Scotland Road, Shaw Street, Moss Street, Hope Street and Mount Pleasant to Lewis's where he will stay until Christmas. He was welcomed on his arrival by Mr F. Hope, general manager of Lewis's.

November 10th

1886: Local hooligans caused mayhem at a race meeting at Aintree and carried out a serious assault. The violence was carried out by 'cornermen', a term given to groups who loitered about or roamed around intimidating others into giving them money for beer. As the *Liverpool Mercury* put it:

Yesterday the violence of the Liverpool Cornermen was exemplified in a murderous and unprovoked attack made by two ruffians on a young man at the racecourse in Aintree and who now lies at the Bootle Hospital in a very critical condition. Visitors to the Aintree course cannot but notice the increasing amount of roughs who frequent these meetings. To even a casual observer an unusually large number of these roughs were yesterday present, many of them carrying heavy sticks, dangerous looking implements in the hands of their possessors. About two o'clock a most dangerous affray occurred in a remote but crowded part of the arena. A number of disreputable looking young fellows, most of them carrying sticks, were there assembled. Two of them were seen to be addressing a few words to a young man who was standing near the railings and then attack him. He fell and the cry was heard that he had been stabbed. His assailants were in the grip of two men who were undoubtedly police officers in plain clothes.

NOVEMBER 11TH

1918: There were jubilant scenes throughout Liverpool following news that an armistice had been signed with Germany, bringing to an end four years of hostilities. It was a mild day for the time of year: the sun shone and there was hardly any wind. As news began to seep through that fighting would cease at 11 a.m., excitement grew. The *Evening Express* reported:

> The Lord Mayor immediately on receipt of the news at once ordered the flag to be flown at the mast of the civic mission. The Lord Mayor appeared on the balcony and asked people to keep cool and carry on. And from this moment the city began to be beside itself with joy. In a moment it seemed that the message of peace had penetrated every corner of the city's commercial heart, for out of the buildings people poured and the streets were flooded with a seething mass of humanity.

Men in factories and the docks had been allowed to leave work and on the River Mersey, ships claxons made a deafening sound. Hawkers did a roaring trade selling flags to revellers on the streets. The *Evening Express* said that there was a particularly good reception for soldiers, saying: 'Three wounded Tommies wrapped in a huge flag received a good reception. Officers were seen riding on the roofs of taxi cabs and cheering as they sped through the street.'

NOVEMBER 12TH

1899: The 13th Hussars cavalry regiment sailed from Liverpool for South Africa to fight in the Boer War. The war with the Boers, Dutch settlers in South Africa, had broken out two weeks earlier and the Hussars were part of a force being sent out to end the siege of Ladysmith.

They were due to set sail on the 10th but were delayed by inclement weather. On 13 November the *Liverpool Mercury* reported of their departure: 'The Johnston Line Transporter Templemore sailed yesterday. As she proceeded down the Mersey the whistles of numerous steamers were sounded and the passengers on board the numerous ferry boats cheered and waved their handkerchiefs.'

The 13th Hussars disembarked at Durban on 5 December and Ladysmith was finally relieved on 1 March.

NOVEMBER 13TH

1987: A lighting strike by train guards caused chaos at Lime Street station. The background to the strike was judicial: twelve employees were under suspension for an alleged ticket fraud which was due to be heard by the magistrates' court. The previous day nine of these were dismissed, angering guards (who felt they had been judged by their employers before having a chance to appear before a court). The walkout began at 8.15 a.m. on a Friday morning and was to last until midnight. The *Liverpool Echo* reported that evening: 'Bewildered businessmen and weekend travellers were among thousands who were left marooned for hours at Lime Street Station as one in two trains were stranded without guards. Tempers flared amongst travellers as dozens of services were cancelled.'

Things got worse for travellers – and there was even more bad luck for one unfortunate businessman who left his briefcase, containing a computer, unattended, leading to it being blown up during a controlled explosion: 'The bomb scare in the evening added to the chaos. Travellers loaded with suitcases were evacuated from the station for an hour and a half whilst experts blew up the suspicious package.'

NOVEMBER 14TH

1860: The funeral took place of Catherine (Kitty) Wilkinson, founder of the wash house.

Originally from Ireland, Wilkinson opened up her cellar for residents to wash clothes during the cholera epidemic of 1832, as hers was the only boiler in the street, charging 1*d* a time. Developing this concept, she went on to establish proper wash houses, the first opening in Upper Frederick Street in 1842. She also took in many of the town's orphans, ensuring they were fed, washed and taught. On 13 November a letter to the *Liverpool Mercury* paid tribute, describing her as: 'Remarkably unrequiring and reserved, in truly Samaritan and Christian spirit her efforts to relieve knew no limits but in a power to serve.'

She was buried in St James' Cemetery, and her funeral was attended by people from all walks of life. Her gravestone carried the inscription: 'Indefatigable and self denying, she was the widows' friend, the support of the orphan, the fearless and the unwanted. Nurse of the sick, the originator of baths and wash houses for the poor.'

Wilkinson has been honoured by a stained glass window in Liverpool Cathedral.

NOVEMBER 15TH

1968: Police in Merseyside appealed for help from the public in combatting crime in the Christmas shopping rush. The *Liverpool Echo* reported the launch of 'an all-out campaign against shoplifters and pickpockets' by the Liverpool and Bootle Police during the Christmas shopping rush. 'Each year,' it continued, 'thousands of pounds worth of goods disappear from city stores in the busy weeks before the holiday.'

Chief Constable James Haughton explained how the public could help and had a warning to opportunists:

Extra vigilance by counter assistants is obviously necessary at this time. Shoppers can assist by reporting any suspicious behaviour. Christmas time, when people are hampered by parcels, makes any store a happy hunting-ground for pickpockets and petty thieves. Woman shoppers in particular should be careful with purses and handbags. Every year we have these personal tragedy stories of women losing their Christmas shopping money and this means that many children are disappointed. There is also the other personal tragedy of when people submit to personal temptation and steal from shops. Many of them are arrested and taken to court and their lives are ruined because of one moment's folly.

NOVEMBER 16TH

1898: There was a great interest at the magistrates' court as three Liverpool FC players appeared to answer charges. George Allan, John Walker and Hugh Morgan had all been arrested at midnight the previous Saturday after a policeman heard them arguing in the street on Oakfield Road. After initially refusing to move on, Allan was arrested for 'Using Language Likely to Lead to a Breach of the Peace'; when Walker and Morgan intervened they were arrested for the same offence, with the additional charge of 'Obstructing a Constable'.

The next day's *Liverpool Mercury* reported that during the hearing the police constable denied making insulting remarks to the players for being Scottish, but admitted he took Allan to the Bridewell without telling him his charge. The Stipendiary Magistrate dismissed the case, saying: 'The defendants were all sober and would not have been charged if they had gone away when first ordered... The Stipendiary advised them to turn in earlier on Saturday nights and not to make any more rows in the streets.' There was a coda: 'As many of the defendants friends were leaving the court conversing loudly, they were reminded they were not on a football ground.'

NOVEMBER 17TH

1576: The eighteenth anniversary of Queen Elizabeth's accession to the throne was celebrated. The *Liverpool Town Book* records:

This year the 17th day of November 1576 and entering upon the 19th year of the reign of our most gracious sovereign Lady Elizabeth, by the Grace of God, Queen of England, France and Ireland, Defender of the Faith etc, Master Thomas Bavande, being Mayor of this Majesty's Corporation and port town of Liverpool in the county of Lancaster, caused the same day in the evening a great bonfire to be made in the market place near to the High Cross of the same town, which was done accordingly. And immediately his brethren the aldermen and divers others of the burgess of the same town and so went altogether to the house of Ralph Burscough Alderman, where they banqueted a certain time. Which done, Master Mayor departed to his own house, accompanied of the said aldermen and others, a great number, upon which he did bestow sacke and other white wine and sugar liberally. Standing all without the dore, lauding and praising God for the most prosperous reign of our said most gracious sovereign lady the Queen most excellent Majesty whom God grant long over us to reign with great tranquillity and victorious success over all her graces enemies. And so appointing his bailiffs and other officers to see the fires quenched, departed and went in.

NOVEMBER 18TH

1983: Medical history was made in Liverpool as the world's first surviving female sextuplets were born. The girls, weighing between 2lbs 1oz and 2lbs 15oz, were born by Caesarean section to Graham and Janet Walton of Wallasey, who were undergoing their thirteenth attempt at fertility treatment. Initially they had been told to expect triplets, then five babies, and finally, three weeks before the birth, the number was confirmed at six. The *Liverpool Echo* reported the next day:

> The delighted father of sextuplets born in Liverpool told the world today 'they're smashing'. He had just been paying a visit to the intensive care unit at Liverpool's Oxford Street Maternity Hospital where the girls are doing just fine in incubators. When asked if he was having any more children he laughed 'not at the moment'.

The odds against the birth were more than three billion to one. The consultant paediatrician described the infants: 'The babies were not identical: they differed in facial expression, size and hair colouring, which ranges from pale mousey to quite dark.' He said three of the babies were breathing normally and had been taken off respirators. The sextuplets continue to receive media interest and have been the subject of several television documentaries.

NOVEMBER 19TH

1975: A row broke out in Liverpool City Council over the obscene content of some library books.

The *Liverpool Echo* reported Liberal councillor Jim Gallagher's belief that children were being exposed to 'mental arson', and that certain books needed to be censored or removed from the shelves as they were worse than anything available in 'wartime Port Said'. However, the city's librarian told the Library and Leisure Committee:

> If books were freely available in the shops then it was difficult to keep them out of the public library. People have come back with a book and said, 'this book is filthy: it should be taken off the shelf'. I have had to say that I couldn't restrict the use of the book no matter what my personal feelings were. If a book has been published and is freely available then I cannot restrict its use.

NOVEMBER 20TH

1944: A fire at Allerton golf course severely damaged its historic clubhouse. The clubhouse was built by Jacob Fletcher in 1815 as a mansion house called Allerton; the estate was taken over by Liverpool Corporation in 1924 to be turned into a municipal golf course. The following day's *Daily Post* reported that the fire began in an upstairs office and was discovered by Mrs Large, wife of the club professional Mr W. Large. Efforts were made to tackle the fire using buckets of water but they couldn't prevent its spreading rapidly.

'A number of valuable paintings on the ground floor on loan from the Walker Art Galley' said the *Post*, 'were saved. Several civilians formed a chain to salvage golfing equipment from a shop on the ground floor. The locker rooms upstairs which contained about 100 golf clubs, all privately owned, were completely destroyed.'

The work of the fire brigade was not helped by the inadequate water supplies by the clubhouse, forcing them to run hoses hundreds of yards to Mather Avenue to get more. Due to the extent of the damage, the stables were converted into a new clubhouse. The mansion house still stands but is not in use.

NOVEMBER 21ST

1955: Rumours broke that Everton FC were interested in taking over South Liverpool FC's Holly Park ground. South Liverpool, based in Garston on the site of what is now Liverpool South Parkway station, was the city's premier non-league club, but it was in financial difficulty. The team rented their ground from Liverpool Corporation, and in that evening's *Liverpool Echo* football columnist 'Ranger' suggested Everton might be interested in it, reporting:

> For the past few weeks unofficial talks have been taking place about Everton taking over the lease of Holly Park. When I made inquiries about this last Friday I was told there was nothing further to report and the moves were unofficial and purely tentative.

A similar move had been made ten years earlier, with Everton proposing to play 'A' team games at Holly Park, but it was rejected by South shareholders. A South official said: 'We have no comment to make at this stage, we have had no communication from Everton either by word of mouth or letter.' The move never came about and South struggled on at Holly Park for another thirty-five years before leaving due to vandalism. They are currently playing at Jericho Lane in Aigburth in the West Cheshire League, a far lower level than they used to play at.

NOVEMBER 22ND

1967: Local radio came to Liverpool when the first broadcast was made by Radio Merseyside. The station was the third BBC local radio station to launch, following on from Radio Leicester and Radio Sheffield which began broadcasting earlier in the month. The *Liverpool Echo* reported that evening:

> BBC Radio Merseyside opened transmissions today with an infectious jingle composed by Liverpool pop star Gerry Marsden. I guarantee it will be an immediate hit with listeners. Transmissions began with an outside broadcast by Vic Marmion from the Wallasey excavations for the second Mersey tunnel. Radio Merseyside broadcast goodwill messages from the Post-master General, from its sister stations in Leicester and Sheffield, and from the Mayor of another Liverpool – in Nova Scotia. In his message the Post-master General said the programmes must always be 'with it', must never be dull and above all must be tailor-made for Merseyside.

Radio Merseyside is still going strong and one of the most popular regional stations.

NOVEMBER 23RD

1915: Details were announced of how much money had been collected locally by the Prince of Wales National Relief Fund, set up for wounded soldiers. The *Daily Post* and *Mercury* said the following day:

Mr Percy Corkhill (Lord Mayor's Secretary) gave some interesting details concerning the collection of the local Prince of Wales Fund, the highest sum ever raised for philanthropic purposes in this city. Up to September 20th the people of Liverpool had raised £157,903 19s 11d, a record of which the city might be justly proud. Some very large donations were given by sympathisers: for example, one citizen subscribed £13,000 to the local fund and £5,000 to the national fund. As many as 237 firms had contributed without intermission since the start of the fund. They appealed for regular subscriptions, weekly or monthly, which were the backbone of the fund.

NOVEMBER 24TH

1907: There was a tragedy at the Sailors' Home in Canning Place when a policeman was killed after the gate fell on top of him. The *Liverpool Daily Courier* reported next day of the incident:

> A distressing tragedy occurred to a Liverpool policeman named Brownlow Locke in the early hours of Sunday morning. Locke was on duty in the neighbourhood of the Sailors' Home and at about five to one the porter of that institution set about closing the establishment, the front entrance of which is guarded by iron gates running in a groove. In consequence of an obstruction one of the gates weighing about 15cwt stuck and the constable went to the porter's assistance to lift it into the proper position. Their united energies resulted in the gate being moved but owing to something at present unexplained it became released from its fastenings and fell upon the constable, who was knocked to the ground and terribly crushed.

Constable Locke was taken to the Royal Southern Hospital where he died an hour after arrival of a fractured skull and severe internal injuries. He left a widow and one child.

After spending many years in a museum in the West Midlands, the gates of the Sailors' Home returned to the city in 2011 and stand in Paradise Street as a memorial to merchant seamen who passed through the city.

NOVEMBER 25TH

1932: At the Annual General Meeting of Walker Cains Brewery, an interesting light was put on the beer tax. Walker Cains had been formed in 1921 by the merger of Liverpool-based Cains and Warrington's Peter Walker. The chairman of the company told members that although the chancellor was raising revenue from increased taxes on beer, more was being lost as it only led to a fall in profits for breweries. The *Evening Express* reported:

> Sir Charles A. Nall-Cain, moving the report, said in reference to the additional tax of 31s per barrel of beer, the Chancellor had collected from their three breweries during the last year £204 more than for the year ending September 1931, when the lower rate of duty was in operation. The combined results of their two principal companies showed a decreased profit of £214,000. The chancellor would therefore next year receive over £50,000 less for income tax, to say nothing of the reduced amount of super-tax received from shareholders.

NOVEMBER 26TH

1866: A ship was lost at the entrance to the River Mersey, with the loss of all its crew. The *Elizabeth Buckham* had sailed from Demerara in South America two months earlier with a cargo of rum, coconuts and sugar. She struck rocks at Burbo Bank in heavy seas at about 10 p.m. On 28 November the *Liverpool Mercury* reported:

> Another sad shipwreck with loss of life off the port has to be reported. The ill-fated vessel was the brigantine *Elizabeth Buckham*. Though observed by the steam tug *Rattler* no assistance could be rendered. She beat upon the bank and speedily went to pieces, the whole of her crew, pilot included, perishing. All day yesterday the beach at New Brighton and coast up to Crosby were strewn with wrecks from her, the marks of which placed the vessel's identity beyond doubt.

The captain, pilot and crew of about twelve all perished. Two more died at New Brighton in the following days when they were swept away by the tide, having fallen asleep after drinking rum that had washed ashore.

NOVEMBER 27TH

1920: There was a spate of arson attacks on the Liverpool and Bootle docks, with the IRA believed to be responsible. The Irish War of Independence was on-going in Ireland, and towards the end of 1920 the campaign spread to the mainland, with attacks also taking place in the North East and London.

In Liverpool, shots were fired at police and there were six fires in just a two-and-a-half-hour period, with a further nine at Bootle:

> The fires broke out simultaneously at about nine o'clock and so serious were some of them that firemen were on duty all night and far into yesterday. Cotton warehouses and timber yards were chosen for destruction. Great quantities of paraffin were used by the incendiaries who gained admittance to the warehouses and timber yards by cutting padlocks with powerful bolt clippers. In Bootle the Military are guarding the docks and in Liverpool the Chief Constable informed us last night the public can be assured that every precaution is being taken. There have been five arrests. Some of the men detained were associated with people associated with the local Sinn Fein movement.

> (The *Daily Post and Mercury*)

NOVEMBER 28TH

1947: It was announced that Liverpool Cathedral – along with several local services – was a beneficiary of the will of the Countess of Sefton, who had died on 27 August at the age of seventy-two. The *Evening Express* reported:

> The Right Hon. Helena Mary, Countess of Sefton, Bridge House, Mossley Hill Drive, Liverpool, widow of the 6th Earl of Sefton and daughter of the 4th Earl of Bradford, left £73,851 gross (net £70,389), duty paid £19,078. She left £200 to Liverpool Cathedral building fund, £100 to 'the scheme which I inaugurated with the British Legion Liverpool for the help of disabled ex-servicemen', £100 each to the Heswall Open Air Hospital for children and the Royal Lancaster Infirmary, £50 to the Women's Service Bureau Liverpool, [and] £25 to the horses' home of rest, Liverpool. £50 each to Evelyn Furnell Valerie Holmes Percy and Charlie Gibbins, in recognition of their father's long and faithful service. After several other legacies the residue goes to her son the Earl of Sefton, of Croxteth Hall, Liverpool.

NOVEMBER 29TH

1910: The first known flight of an airplane across the River Mersey took place. The flight in a two-seater plane was piloted by local aviator Compton Paterson of the Liverpool Motor House Co., based in Freshfields. His passenger was Mr R.A. King, one of his pupils. They had put the plane together after it was transported from the Farman works in France. The *Liverpool Mercury* reported the following day:

Yesterday a clever exhibition of flying was given in the Mersey district, the sphere of aerial movement being Freshfield, New Brighton, Hoylake and back. The start was shortly before two o'clock and New Brighton was made in a few minutes, Mr King being the first aerial passenger ever being ferried across. They proceeded to Hoylake, landing across from the golf course. The machine worked splendidly and the two passengers reached a height of 500 feet above the Mersey. The machine, after returning from Hoylake, vol-planed down the sands at New Brighton behind the lighthouse and the marine park. Immediately the machine was heard coming along great crowds flocked to the sands and Mr Paterson explained the machine to all inquisitors. After a short stay the two men got into the machine which rose with delicate grace then steered a straight line across the Mersey towards Freshfield.

NOVEMBER 30TH

1618: Richard Mather preached his first sermon at the newly built chapel in Toxteth.

Mather, a former teacher at the Puritan school in Toxteth had been away at Oxford University whilst the chapel was being built. According to an account of Mather's life published anonymously in New England in 1670, recounted in Valentine Davis's *Some Account of the Ancient Chapel of Toxteth Park* in 1883: 'There was a very great concourse of people to hear him and his labours were highly accepted of by the judicious. Such was the vastness of his memory as that the things which he had prepared and intended to deliver at once contained no less than six long sermons.'

Mather was a Minister at Toxteth for fifteen years before moving to become a pastor in New England. The Ancient Chapel of Toxteth, as it has been for some time, is still in existence as a Unitarian chapel.

DECEMBER 1ST

1865: Compton House, Liverpool's largest department store, was destroyed by fire. The five-storey emporium on the corner of Basnett Street and Church Street had only recently been expanded but was completely destroyed, gutted in a fire so great that the *Liverpool Daily Courier* commented the next day: 'However far the memory may be carried back, it will fail to find a fire of the same magnitude as illuminated Liverpool last night.' The fire began between around nine o'clock and took about an hour to gain a hold. Reinforcements were brought in from as far away as West Derby to help fight the fire, while the crew of HMS *Donegal* also gave assistance. Describing the scene, the *Courier* wrote:

> The whole of the Church Street front was in a glow and flames of intense brilliancy and enormous volume were spouting from every window and the roof. The crowd had assembled in their thousands in Church Street. The light from the burning pile was so intense that the people, had they so chosen, might have been able to read the smallest print as easily as by the full glare of the noonday sun.

Compton House was re-built and re-opened two years later but never did as well as before, closing in 1871. Marks & Spencer now occupies the building.

DECEMBER 2ND

1955: On this day Mabel Fletcher, Liverpool's first female Alderman and longest serving female councillor, died.

She died after a month-long illness in Fazakerley Hospital and that evening's *Liverpool Echo* paid tribute to her as follows:

Miss Fletcher, a member of the council since 1919, became an alderman in 1930 representing County ward. She was also one of Liverpool's first women magistrates, being appointed in 1920. At her own request she was placed on the retired list in 1948. Though she rarely spoke in the council chamber Miss Fletcher was a hard working member of many committees. Until last May, when Labour took control of the City Council she was chair of the Special Services Sub-Committee of the Education Committee and she had also served on the Housing, Highways and Planning, Libraries, Public Assistance and Health Committees, among others. In 1949 to mark her long service to education in the city, the Wavertree Technical School for girls was re-named the Mabel Fletcher Technical College. Last year the Liverpool University conferred upon her the honorary degree of MA. Miss Fletcher, who lived at the Adelphi hotel, was in her eightieth year.

DECEMBER 3RD

1983: A teddy bears' picnic held at St Peter's church in Woolton raised over £1,000 for charity. The event was special in that the teddy bears present were donated by celebrities, politicians and sports stars. The *Liverpool Echo* reported on 5 December:

'Top people's teddy bears from all over the country were at a money spinning picnic in Liverpool on Saturday. Margaret Thatcher's teddy bear rubbed shoulders with Princess Anne's at St Peter's church hall, Woolton, to raise cash for a children's charity. The 153 names on the guest list for the event, which raised more than £1,000 for the NSPCC, including the favourites of the Duke of Westminster, Marquis of Bath and Countess Mountbatten. Also putting their bears on show were show business stars Cilla Black, Sir Harry Seacombe, Richard Briers and Paul Daniels. Stars of Liverpool FC also allowed their bears to be used for the day, as well as MPs including Enoch Powell and Dr David Owen. The show was organised by the *Echo* and promoted by the NSPCC as part of a nationwide campaign to raise £100,000 in their centenary year.

DECEMBER 4TH

1848: SFX church in Everton – or the church of St Francis Xavier, to give it its full name – was opened. The church was built following a meeting of eight Catholic business men at the Rose & Crown pub eight years earlier, who pledged to build a Catholic church to be handed to the Jesuits.

Poor weather meant the attendance was not as great as could have been, but the event went well:

> This splendid edifice, situated in Salisbury Street opposite the Collegiate Institution, was opened for Divine service yesterday. The sermon was preached by the Rev. William Cobb. He delivered with great eloquence a panegyric upon the saint whose name has been given the church. After the service all the clergy and a number of ladies and gentlemen were most hospitably entertained at the house attached to the church by the Rev. Francis West. (*Liverpool Mercury*)

SFX went on to become the largest Catholic parish in England after the Second World War. In the 1980s it was under threat after slum clearance in the area but was saved after a nationwide campaign.

DECEMBER 5TH

1805: Services of Thanksgiving were held in Liverpool to commemorate Britain's victory in the Battle of Trafalgar. The battle, fought against Spanish and French forces off the south west coast of Spain on 21 October, had ensured Britain's naval superiority and staved off the threat of invasion. The 5 December was declared a national Thanksgiving Day, and services were to be held and collections taken for the relief of wounded soldiers and widows.

Gore's General Advertiser stated that day:

> A collection for the relief of widows and orphans of those brave men who gloriously fell in the late naval action will be held at St George's church immediately after Divine service this Thanksgiving Day (this forenoon). This evening a collection will be made at the Dissenters' Chapel in Byrom Street in aid of the Patriotic Fund, for the relief of widows and children of those who have fallen in defence of their country and a sermon will be preached by the Rev. Richard Davis.

The following week's edition of Gore's reported that just under £2,000 had been pledged in Liverpool's churches, a phenomenal sum for the time.

DECEMBER 6TH

1922: A carnival and bazaar in aid of the Liverpool Children's Hospital opened at St George's Hall which aimed to reduce a £30,000 overdraft:

> The Marchioness of Aberdeen and Tamair said no cause was worthy of greater support than that of curing the sick child. Liverpool was an example to others in the welfare of caring for sick children, both in the matter of school inspection and their many wonderful institutions for curing sick children. Sir Thomas Royden, who was accompanied by Lady Royden, presided, and a vote of thanks to the Marchioness was proposed by Mr Alfred Holt, Chairman of the carnival and bazaar. The Marchioness was also presented with a beautiful bouquet of roses by little Miss Eileen Chimes. (*Evening Express*)

DECEMBER 7TH

1970: A one-off television play, *The Onedin Line*, was shown on BBC1, based on a shipping family in Victorian Liverpool. Written by Cyril Abraham, it was broadcast at 9.50 p.m. and was published in the television listings of that evening's *Liverpool Echo* as: 'DRAMA PLAYHOUSE – *The Onedin Line*. A hundred years ago all a man needed to make a fortune was a ship, the courage to sail her and the cunning to survive in a cut throat business. Stars Peter Gilmore, Edward Chapman, James Hayter.'

The one-off production was so well received that a fifteen episode series was commissioned, first broadcast in October 1971. It eventually ran until 1980, eight series in all. Despite being set in Liverpool, all the filming was done in Devon, with Dartmouth substituting for Liverpool docks.

In September 2010 the original playhouse recording was re-discovered in the American Library of Congress. Also in 2010, digital television channel 'Yesterday' began transmitting all of the series' episodes.

DECEMBER 8TH

1926: A touch of rural England came to Liverpool with a cattle show in Haymarket. The show was held by the Liverpool & District Cattle Association. Despite Liverpool being an urban area, those attending maintained that the quality of milk produced by local cattle was still good, as the *Evening Express* reported that day:

> Dr Gullen, in his presidential address, said the show had a far reaching effect, for it meant that members of the association were working to producing the best milk. 'The cattle in this show', he added 'is the finest in England and I defy any show in the country, even Smithfield, to produce better fat cattle or dairy cattle. Alderman Muirhead said that although the number of cattle kept in Liverpool shippons was lower than in 1914, the quality of the milk was better.

Awards were won by cattle farmers from Aigburth, Bootle, Roby and Waterloo. George Holding, from Bury, who had been judging the cattle for twenty-one years, was presented with a silver tea tray in recognition.

DECEMBER 9TH

1874: A bridewell keeper was cleared at the magistrates' court of an allegation that he had committed a serious assault on a prisoner. The Liverpool *Daily Albion* reported the following day:

Thomas Higgins, a booking clerk, employed at the Rose-hill Bridewell, was charged by an elderly respectable looking woman named Julia Cartister, with committing a criminal assault. On Sunday evening the Prosecutrix was booked at the Rose-hill Bridewell on a charge of being drunk and incapable and was placed in a cell alone. The charge against the defendant, who was on duty at the bridewell that night, was that while she was in the cell he committed a violent and criminal assault upon her. Evidence showed that the woman was very drunk and she admitted that she had been several times previously in the custody of the police and had been fined by the magistrates. She could not swear to the defendant, but said that it was a man with a red waistcoat who assaulted her, and the defendant was the only man wearing a red waistcoat who was present at the bridewell that night. The magistrates did not think there was sufficient evidence to warrant them in committing the defendant for trial and accordingly the summons was dismissed.

DECEMBER 10TH

1962: The Palladium cinema in West Derby Road was only saved from being gutted by fire thanks to the fortunate presence of a policeman in the area.

The fire in the deserted building was discovered at 12.35 a.m. by a constable who was on patrol in the area. The fire brigade quickly arrived at the scene to put it under control, limiting damage to the top of a balcony staircase. The *Liverpool Echo* on that day stated that the cinema would be closed for a few days but that the damage could have been a lot worse. The manager said: 'Had it not been for the remarkably quick work of the fire service there would not have been a Palladium at all in another ten minutes.'

Despite its lucky escape the Palladium lasted less than five more years. It was closed and demolished in 1967 to make way for a road-widening scheme.

DECEMBER 11TH

1949: The Cunard liner *Britannic* docked in Liverpool, carrying gifts from the crew which were to be distributed at Liverpool Children's Hospital. The ship had arrived from New York, where crew members had spent their own money on toys and Christmas cake ingredients especially for children at the hospital. The *Daily Post* reported the following day that a crew member had told them: 'We bought $36 worth of toys for the children in New York. At the same time we chased around for Christmas cake ingredients and the cake was baked on the homeward trip.'

The *Post* revealed that the Brooklyn British Merchant Navy Club had also sent a private consignment of gifts to the hospital, situated in Myrtle Street. The captain of the ship, R.G. Theldwell, commented: 'It's nice to know that the crew have sacrificed some of their pay – and the few dollars they're allowed – to make other people's children happy.'

DECEMBER 12TH

1925: Twenty-five members of Liverpool's Chinese community appeared in court after being arrested for illegal gaming. That evening's *Evening Express* reported:

> 25 Chinamen who were arrested in a raid at a house in Pitt Street in Liverpool on Saturday appeared before the Liverpool Stipendiary at Dale Street Police Court today. Mr Howard Roberts, prosecuting, said that the house was apparently a tobacconist's shop but actually there was no business except gaming. The cigarette packets in the window were dummies. The police found dominoes for money being played in two rooms on the ground floor. The men alleged to be assisting were acting as either bankers or manipulators. A detective sergeant said that in the window there was a notice in Chinese characters indicating, 'This establishment is now open for gaming', and passers-by could see it.

Three of the men were fined and twenty others were bound over not to frequent gaming houses.

DECEMBER 13TH

1958: Shoppers on the penultimate Saturday before Christmas faced weather and transport problems. The *Liverpool Echo* reported that night: 'Snow, sleet and rain on Merseyside today made conditions unpleasant for Christmas shoppers. As they alighted from buses snow was falling and there was a true Christmassy atmosphere. Many had come unprepared for the sudden change in weather and there was a demand in the shop for plastic mackintoshes.'

Store managers reported that there was a high demand for toy cars and musical greetings cards. Extra buses were laid on, although the Corporation still advised that queues should be expected between 4 p.m. and 6 p.m. Those driving were faced with heavy queues, the *Echo* stating that:

After midday traffic in the city centre, particularly in the Church Street, Lord Street, Paradise Street area became particularly heavy. For motorists it was a case of stop, crawl, crawl, stop. One motorist who left Victoria Street to travel to Paradise Street said it took him ten minutes to make a journey that would normally take two minutes. Through the diesel and petrol fumes, crowds of shoppers swept in one mass across the road seeking the rare gaps in the traffic queues to reach the opposite pavement.

DECEMBER 14TH

1980: A vigil was held at St George's Plateau to remember John Lennon, gunned down in New York six days earlier. Bands including Gerry and the Pacemakers performed on a stage in a concert organised by former Beatles impresario Sam Leach. Then, at 7 p.m., there was a ten-minute silent vigil, which was being observed by Lennon fans worldwide at the request of his widow, Yoko Ono. The next day's *Daily Post* reported:

> 25,000 paid a final tribute in Liverpool last night in memory of the man of peace. Many had spent all night outside St George's Hall in freezing conditions in readiness for music and prayer. After the candlelit vigil, hundreds joined arms and sang Lennon's famous anti-war anthem 'Give Peace a Chance'.

A wreath was laid on the door of St George's Hall with the inscription 'John Winston Lennon RIP, a great lad who put our town on the map'. The vigil was led by David Arnott, chaplain of Liverpool Polytechnic (which had absorbed the art college where Lennon spent two years as a student).

Thirty years later, another vigil was held at Chavasse Park and a peace monument was unveiled in Lennon's honour.

DECEMBER 15TH

1976: Merseyside Police's campaign against Christmas drink drivers began:

If you are going to the office party this Christmas, don't drink and drive, motorists were warned today. Partygoers throughout Merseyside face a breath test blitz and police intend to put every available man on traffic duty to swoop on drink-drive motorists. Merseyside's Traffic Chief Superintendent Eric Wright gave the grim warning: 'My men won't hesitate to pull up any driver who looks as though he's had too many. The public can rest assured about that,' he said. People who ignore this warning will lose their licences, perhaps even their livelihoods. Then there are others who won't live to regret it. (*Liverpool Echo*)

DECEMBER 16TH

1931: The Liverpool Coroner called for action against Christmas tontine clubs after the suicide of a local treasurer. The forty-year-old woman from Kirkdale had run a tontine club, but also lent money using its proceeds (charging interest of 1*d* a week). After she experienced difficulty in getting back the money she was owed, she gassed herself in her kitchen a week before the tontine was due to pay out.

The *Evening Express* that day reported that whilst recording a verdict of 'Suicide While of Unsound Mind', the coroner Mr G. C. Mort stated:

> Every Christmas I get a series of these suicides and I think something should be done about it. It is obvious that this unfortunate woman traded in an honest manner and has been done down. She was not a responsible person to be lending money. She could not afford to take a law action against people who did not pay it back. I should like to know whereby this scheme is illegal whereby money subscribed to a tontine club is lent at interest. If it is illegal something should be done by the police to prevent it.

Regarding the Coroner's comments a police sergeant said that as the interest on the money lent was to be shared amongst members and the woman was getting no financial gain she did not come under the Moneylenders Act.

DECEMBER 17TH

1896: Liverpool felt the effects of one of the most powerful earthquakes ever to hit the UK. The quake, which occurred at 5.35 a.m., had Hereford as its epicentre and measured 5.3 on the Richter Scale. It was the strongest to hit the UK in the nineteenth century, and there have only been three stronger ones since. The following day's *Liverpool Mercury* stated: 'Although local earthquake shocks have not been hitherto unknown there has rarely been if ever any visitation of these phenomena so widespread and unmistakeable as were reported yesterday from many parts of England and Wales.'

The paper reported that operating boards in the Liverpool telephone exchange were violently shaken and that:

> The sudden terrestrial shock was almost the sole topic of conversation in Liverpool during the day, [and] for some seconds windows shook violently. The crew of the tugboat *Brocklebank*, which was lying at anchor on the river off Herculaneum Dock, report that just as they were hauling up their anchor they received a very severe shaking.

The *Mercury* predicted that further shocks might follow, although these never materialised.

DECEMBER 18TH

1895: Messrs Watts & Co. a draper's based in Compton House, invited children to attend their Christmas grotto:

Messrs Watts & Co. have pleasure in informing their friends the children, the parents of the Greater Liverpool that is to be, that Father Christmas is at COMPTON HOUSE THIS DAY, at ten o'clock this morning. He is accompanied by lions, tigers, wolves, bears, jackals, camels, dromedaries, zebras, giraffes, antelope, reindeer, bison, elks, buffaloes, jaguars, pumas, leopards, apes, monkeys, gorillas, baboons, the cassowary of Timbuctoo, elephants, kangaroos, mustangs, Jerusalem and Shetland ponies, the dinotherium, the ichtyosauras, the labyrinthodon, the megatherium, the great auk and the dodo – in fact, with a complete Noah's Ark, containing all the original animals and a few others invented, perfected or improved by Professor Huxley, and a real genuine and original water baby. ENTRANCE TO COMPTON HOUSE FREE, ENTRANCE TO THE GROTTO SIXPENCE. In exchange for which Father Christmas, or one of his attendant fairies, elves, brownies, pixies, gnomes or sprites will give every good boy or girl who visits him A BUMPER PACKET OF TOYS fresh from Fairyland, worth its weight in… well wait till you see it!! (*Liverpool Mercury*)

DECEMBER 19TH

1898: The Bishop of London gave an address at St George's Hall, as part of the celebration of the centenary of the Athenaeum Club.

The club was formed for the gentlemen of the town to have somewhere where up-to-date newspapers and books were available. To celebrate the centenary the club put on display at its premises in Church Street a collection of books, as well as maps and directories, illustrating the growth of Liverpool, and bound copies of newspapers. The Bishop's address, described by the *Liverpool Mercury* the following day as 'pleasant and stimulating', focused on differences in education at the end of the nineteenth century compared to when the Athenaeum was formed:

> A despairing contrast [exists] between the conception of study formed by the founders of the institution 100 years ago and that which seems to animate the practice of society today. Now we do not read good books, we do not pursue any systematic course of study: we prefer to acquire omniscient ignorance by snippets. This appetite has been fed by manuals, handbooks and worse of all, by scrappy journals and magazines.

Today the club is still in operation, having moved to Church Alley in 1924 after Church Street was widened, its membership being limited to 500.

DECEMBER 20TH

1940: An air-raid on Liverpool led to the deaths of at least seventy-two people when a shelter took a direct hit in Blackstock Gardens, Vauxhall.

The exact number of casualties was never confirmed due to the devastation caused and the fact that it is believed some bodies were washed away in a stream. Whole families were wiped out, and in one instance a mother and six of her children died. Due to wartime reporting restrictions, the full extent was not published in the local media at the time. The following night's *Liverpool Echo*, under the subheading of 'SHELTER STRUCK', could say no more than 'A communal shelter was hit and it is feared that there are many casualties'. For many years afterwards an annual memorial procession took place in the neighbourhood until Blackstock Gardens was demolished in 1968.

In 1998 a memorial was unveiled in Vauxhall Road, listing the names of the seventy-two residents known to have died. It bears the inscription: 'In memory of the residents of Blackstock Gardens that died in an air raid on the 20th/21st December 1940. Also for the unknown, may they rest in peace.'

DECEMBER 21ST

1927: There was a chaotic scene in Liverpool city centre as two elephants broke free from their keepers:

> Two elephants being walked from Central Station to the Olympia Circus in Liverpool today broke from their keepers and dashed about among the crowd of shoppers. One of them tried to enter the Press Club in Lime Street but was baulked by the revolving door. The other is stated to have sat on a wooden crate filled with goods in Elliot Street. Later the front legs of the elephants were shackled and they were safely conveyed to the Olympia.
>
> (*Evening Express*)

Circuses continued at the Olympia until its conversion into a cinema in 1930.

DECEMBER 22ND

1974: Liverpool's dockers worked through the night to unload a shipload of vegetables ensuring supplies would be on the dinner tables for Christmas.

The Aznar Line's *Monte Umbo* arrived from the Canary Islands carrying 1,000,000Ib of tomatoes, 300,000Ib of cucumbers and 150,000Ib of new potatoes. She was the last ship with these vegetables to arrive in the UK before Christmas, and dockers were on standby to begin unloading as soon as she arrived. The *Liverpool Echo* reported that the first lorry-loads of vegetables were on the road to Scotland, Wales and Northern England within an hour, which could only be good news for consumers. It quoted a shipping agent as saying:

> It was a tight timetable and there was a threat that some of the fruit and vegetables might have had to lie in a dock shed over Christmas. From the retailers and housewives standpoint, this would have meant short supplies and higher prices in the shops. We reckon the co-operation of dockers and drivers proves yet again that few ports can serve such a wide area of Britain in such a short time period.

The *Monte Umbo* left Liverpool with no cargo but with 250 passengers who were to enjoy a cruise around the Canaries.

DECEMBER 23RD

1935: The *Daily Post* issued a last-minute appeal for donations to its Goodfellow fund so that as many needy families as possible could receive some Christmas cheer. The *Post*'s appeal stated:

How can we possibly leave any needy Merseyside families hungry for Christmas Day? The thought is too poignant to entertain but today is the last day to avoid such a possibility. The total provided by Goodfellows during the weekend has reached £1,271, this brings the advancing total to £9,397. If this can be repeated today Mr Goodfellow will be able to feed every single family on his list. If you can possibly make a Goodfellow contribution today, please bring it or send it to Mr Goodfellow at the *Daily Post* and *Echo*, Victoria Street, Liverpool 1. Telephone Central 3400. This is positively the last chance!

The *Post* described the contents of the parcels that the 2,898 families on their list would receive. They were beef, tea, Christmas cake, butter, bacon, sausages, sweets, oranges and jam.

DECEMBER 24TH

1914: The children of those involved in war service were given gifts at Bootle Town Hall. The *Evening Express* reported:

Kiddies from all parts of the borough trooped to Bootle Town Hall to receive the toys which had been sent to the Mayoress for the children of the soldiers and the sailors. About 1,500 splendid toys were distributed under the supervision of the Mayor and Mayoress, who were assisted by their two daughters and Paddy Cassady, the latter in the role of Father Christmas. The children came under response of a post card from the Mayoress and in addition to receiving a splendid present each child was given a bag of sweets, the gift of an anonymous donor. The children also received a Christmas card, designed by some of the scholars at the girls' secondary school. Amongst the gifts were a number of articles of clothing and two big dolls brought by the American ship, *Jason*. One of the dolls was especially reserved for a little invalid girl.

DECEMBER 25TH

1945: As Liverpool enjoyed its first peacetime Christmas since 1938, many were forced to go without turkey due to a shortage. The *Daily Post* on 27 December dubbed it the 'hunt for turkeys Christmas', stating that many families had to fall back on chicken, geese and ducks as they refused to pay huge prices demanded for turkeys, reaching as high as £6. Despite the high prices in turkeys, the *Post* reported that:

> There seems no doubt that most families managed to get a good Christmas meal thanks, among other things, to the increase in rations. It would have been sad had matters turned out otherwise, for many ex-servicemen on Merseyside and ex-prisoners of war were having their first Christmas at home for three, four and even five years. It has been on the whole a stay at home Christmas, [as] many hotels in resorts are still requisitioned by Government departments. Many people wished for their first 'peace' Christmas to be spent by their firesides.

A special service at Liverpool Cathedral was well attended, while at the Liverpool Infirmary a carol service was held in the morning and each patient was given a card and gift. Everton FC, who were playing away at Blackpool, took a busload of fans to the game and then to a tea dance afterwards.

DECEMBER 26TH

1910: The pantomime season got underway in Liverpool, with one of the highlights being *Aladdin* at Kelly's Theatre in Paradise Street.

The *Daily Post and Mercury* reported the next day:

The escapades of Aladdin and his wonderful lamp have been made the most of in production both as regards the romance and the humour. A large caste of artistes has been commissioned and the mirth, vocalism and dancing are on an extensive scale. The grotesque features are especially emphasised with the result that laughter is widespread and frequent. There are in all eleven scenes, including 'The Palace of Wonders', a gorgeous spectacle which comes as the climax to the pantomime. Miss Edith St Clare is a captivating Aladdin and gives a splendid lead, both to the gaiety and humour of the entertainment. In the bewitching charge of Miss Lily Lonsdale, the part of Princess Badroulbadour highly recommends itself. Miss Ethel Lonsdale as slave to the lamp is fascinating to a degree. Bob King creditably accounts for the role of Widow Twankey. In the portrayal of The Emperor, George Belrose finds plenty of scope for his ability, both as a vocalist and comedian. Besides the evening performances, there will be frequent matinees during the three weeks of the pantomime.

DECEMBER 27TH

1990: It was boom time for Liverpool stores and shoppers as the post-Christmas sales began. That evening's *Liverpool Echo* said that early indications suggested figures would be up on the previous year:

> It was spend, spend, spend as stores reported a brisk trade to boost hopes of a bumper sales bonanza beating last year's figures. Early birds hunting for snips were queuing outside Marks and Spencer's, Church Street store from 8 a.m., waiting for the doors to open at 9.30 a.m. on the first day of their sale. A spokesman for their store said 'we have been very, very busy since the doors opened. There are sales right across the store and people are going for very good bargains, like men's suits with £40 off. People are buying things all over the place.'

It was just as busy in British Home Stores in Lord Street, with a spokesman from their store telling the *Echo*: 'It got off to a slow start because the weather put people off getting up early but then it really took off. People have been going for winter season clothing which has been reduced and also Christmas gifts that have not sold. There are also special prices in the home-ware department.'

John Driscoll of the Liverpool Stores Committee was optimistic, saying, 'Our forecast is much greater trade than last year and we aim to end the year with a bang.'

December 28th

1957: Stanley abattoir was shut down after an outbreak of Foot and Mouth. Eighteen cases of the disease were found in the abattoir, which was the largest in the north of England, with a further three the following day.

The *Daily Post* reported on 30 December:

> In addition there must be two or three hundred cattle carcasses which must be regarded as suspect because they have been in contact with the affected cattle or been accommodated in the same pens. But Ministry of Agriculture officials last night gave their sanction for the opening of the meat market this morning for the sale of meat which has been passed as fit and killed over the weekend. The tightest possible controls will be enforced to ensure traders don't encroach the slaughterhouse areas while meat is sold.

The *Post* stated that meat supplies should not be overly affected and although there may be a slight rise, this was usual for the season anyway. The abattoir needed to remain closed for two to three weeks for it to be thoroughly closed and disinfected.

DECEMBER 29TH

1964: Liverpool City Police announced that crime figures had fallen in the run up to Christmas. The following day's *Daily Post* reported that Acting Chief Constable H.R. Balmer had attributed the fall to his commando squad, who worked with plain clothes and uniformed police to cut thefts and pickpocketing. The actions saw thefts fall to 540 from 730 in 1963. There was good news too in Bootle, where there was only one major break-in over the Christmas period. Chief Constable Harold Legg told the *Post* that special crime prevention measures had been an outstanding success: 'Shopkeepers helped by keeping goods, particularly those attractive to thieves, out of easy reach when shops were closed and members of the public helped by reporting suspicious incidents. When this degree of co-operation exists crime in the borough can be kept down to reasonable proportions.'